MW00399241

A Companion
to the
Liturgy of the Hours:

Morning and Evening Prayer

A Companion
to the
Liturgy of the Hours:
Morning and Evening Prayer

By
Shirley Darcus Sullivan

CATHOLIC BOOK PUBLISHING CO.
New Jersey

NIHIL OBSTAT: James M. Cafone, M.A., S.T.D.
Censor Librorum

IMPRIMATUR: ✠ Most Rev. John J. Myers, D.D., J.C.D.
Archbishop of Newark

> **For Mary**
> *Mater Thesauri Cordis*
>
> *And there are many hearts to touch,*
> *many souls to embrace.*

ACKNOWLEDGMENTS

Quotations from the nonbiblical texts of the *Liturgy of the Hours* as well as Psalm 95 and the Canticle of the Lamb, © 1974 by International Committee on English in the Liturgy, Inc., Washington, DC. Reproduced with permission. All rights reserved.

Quotations from the biblical readings and canticles of the *Liturgy of the Hours* (except the Gospel Canticles and the Canticle of the Lamb) are taken from the *New American Bible* © 1970 by the Confraternity of Christian Doctrine, Inc., Washington, DC. Used with permission. All rights reserved. No portion of the *New American Bible* may be reprinted without permission in writing from the copyright holder.

Quotations from the Bible that are not part of the *Liturgy of the Hours* are taken from the *New American Bible* © 1970, 1986, 1992 by the Confraternity of Christian Doctrine, Inc., Washington, DC. Reproduced with permission. All rights reserved. No portion of the *New American Bible* may be reprinted without permission in writing from the copyright holder.

Quotations from the Psalms in the *Liturgy of the Hours* (except Psalm 95) © 1963 and published by Collins, London, 1963. Reproduced with permission. All rights reserved.

Quotations from the *Magnificat* and *Benedictus* are taken from the translations of the International Consultation on English Texts.

(T-415)

Preface

The Church has extended an invitation to all people to share each day in its magnificent prayer, the *Liturgy of the Hours*. In earlier ages this prayer had the title of the *Divine Office* and constituted a "duty" *(officium)* to be fulfilled by those under religious vows. In our own time this prayer, made available in many languages, has become a privilege in which all can share.

Yet the *Liturgy of the Hours* is not an easy form of prayer to adopt. Its structure is complicated. Its format is not quickly or easily understood. At first we need a guide in order to understand the sections of the *Hours*. Mastery of the format, however, comes after a certain time and we can with some sense of triumph realize that we can "say" the *Hours*. "Say," yes. On the one hand we can expertly flip to the required sections. We can confidently face even a "5-ribbon" day. We can join enthusiastically with others in a community recitation of the *Hours*.

"Praying" the *Hours*, on the other hand, may be quite a different experience. Most who take up the invitation to share in the *Hours* will very likely say them in private. For people in this situation the *Hours* ideally will enhance their prayer life. There can be, however, a danger of rote repetition in the private recitation of the *Hours*, if carried on faithfully year after year. The *Hours* may come to be more a duty than a source of inspiration. Completion of the *Hours* may seem to be all that is required and to be somehow in itself meritorious. Sometimes too the mind may wander; the heart may be far otherwise engaged. The will may bring about the reading of the words but may not in any measure be captivated and held by the presence of God.

5

What can help us to make the experience of the *Hours* prayerful? This *Companion to the Hours* hopes to show some ways in which this can be done. In its approach it will draw on the rich spirituality of Carmel, especially that of Elizabeth of the Trinity. The book will offer detailed instructions on how its contents can be used to attend the praying of the *Hours*. The discussions of the psalms, canticles, and readings will act as spiritual commentaries and contribute, it is hoped, to the depth and intensity of "praying" the *Hours*.

The present *Companion* will comment on the psalms, canticles and readings in the 4-volume version of the *Liturgy of the Hours* (New York: Catholic Book Publishing Co., 1975), which is the official text for the United States and Canada. This *Companion* should also prove valuable to anyone who is saying the *Liturgy of the Hours* in the format presented by the webpage: www.universalis.com.

Contents

Introduction to the *Companion*

AS we begin to "say" the *Liturgy of the Hours* we encounter a complicated structure. If we focus on *Morning* or *Evening Prayer*, we basically find psalms, canticles, readings, and intercessory prayers made for the whole Church. Our first challenge is to become familiar with these portions of the *Hours* until their structure is completely known and anticipated. Then we can begin to "pray" the *Hours*. In this Companion we will suggest three possible ways which can enhance our praying the *Hours*. These ways are possibilities only, and many other approaches to the *Hours* could similarly make them rich sources of prayer.

What sort of prayer are we seeking? The *Hours* should provide us with an opportunity to enter deeply into God's presence but with a particular focus. Friend is to meet friend. We are to know who we are: human beings redeemed by the blood of Christ and called on a journey to be transformed into his image. But for all of us the way can be long, the progress, slow. Yet Jesus never stops summoning us to change and to grow:[1]

> Behold, I stand at the door and knock. If anyone hears my voice and opens the door, [then] I will enter his house and dine with him, and he with me (Revelation 3:20).

If we are faithful on the road he has laid out for each of us, Jesus promises a new life within the soul. We are no longer to be alone. Instead, deep within, "company" will come and be our companions:

> Whoever loves me will keep my word, and my Father will love him, and we will come to him and make our dwelling with him (John 14:23).

---

[1]All quotations from the Scriptures that are not found in *The Liturgy of the Hours* are taken from the St. Joseph Edition of the *New American Bible* © by Confraternity of Christian Doctrine 1991, 1986, 1970. All quotations from the Scriptures found in *The Liturgy of the Hours* are taken from the *New American Bible* © 1970 by the Confraternity of Christian Doctrine except for the Psalms, which are in the *Grail* version.

The Father and Jesus will come to dwell with us if we love Jesus. Also, there abides in us the "Spirit of truth" (John 14:17). These companions are "with" us. We still retain our identity but they live in us, suffusing us with their gifts of life and holiness.

Growth in prayer can be described as growth in a relationship with God dwelling within. We learn more and more of who the Father is, who Jesus is, and who the Holy Spirit is. We learn more and more about ourselves, what we should affirm in our natures and what could be changed through grace.

As prayer, the *Liturgy of the Hours* can richly foster this growth in relationship. We shall suggest three perspectives that will contribute to the *Hours* becoming a rich source of prayer. These perspectives involve the conscious adoption of particular points of view. Some will be appropriate with certain psalms, canticles, and readings; others, with different ones. These perspectives, as it were, shed rainbows of different colored lights upon the prayers. The colors make the texts radiant in different ways, and we learn more of the deep calling to which, as Christians, we have been summoned.

The first perspective that this *Companion* will suggest is the "Carmelite." From this rich spiritual tradition we will adopt basic truths with which to approach prayer. The second perspective will be that of "direct address." This perspective will enhance the closeness of our relationship with God. The third perspective will be that of "different voices" to be heard in the various texts we read. This perspective will help us to share more fully in the life of Jesus and of his Church.

Carmelite Perspective

Carmelite spirituality has provided many profound and penetrating insights into the nature of the soul and its

²See K. Kavanaugh, OCD and O. Rodriguez, OCD, *The Complete Works of St. Teresa of Avila*, Washington, DC: ICS Publications, 1980, Vol. 2.

spiritual journey. Teresa of Avila describes in detail the intricate structure of the soul in the *Interior Castle*.[2] At the center of the soul God dwells, and the soul, or perhaps more correctly the will, can come, after a long journey, into this divine presence.[3] John of the Cross discusses extensively the ways in which the soul can encounter God within.[4] He focuses on those elements in the human being, such as emotions and desires, which can hinder the soul's capacity for encountering the divine. He analyzes the composition of the soul and shows what within may be valuable for growth in holiness, and what may not.[5] A Carmelite of the nineteenth century, Elizabeth of the Trinity (1880-1906), likewise deeply understood the nature of the soul and the divine indwelling.[6] Her insights into how the Trinity dwells within and her approach to Scripture will contribute to the "Carmelite" perspective adopted in this *Companion*.[7]

Elizabeth of the Trinity teaches that in each soul God dwells. God's presence there is a definite reality, but most people are completely unaware of it. We need inner eyes to see. Unfortunately, for most of us much of the time, our eyes are turned to the outside world. Elizabeth emphasizes one truth: God is within. Our tendency, as we pray, may be to focus our attention on heaven, looking upward and outward. Such a focus may be well and good. But Elizabeth points out: "I have

[3]See studies on the *Interior Castle* (listed in the Bibliography) by Bielecki, Burrows, Dicken, Dubay, Frolick, Howe, Lati, Sackville-West, and Williams. See also my book, *Transformed by Love: The Soul's Journey to God in Teresa of Avila, Elizabeth of the Trinity, and Mother Aloysius of the Blessed Sacrament*, Hyde Park, NY: New City Press, 2002.

[4]See K. Kavanaugh, OCD and O. Rodriguez, OCD, *The Complete Works of St. John of the Cross*, 2nd ed., Washington, DC: ICS Publications, 1991.

[5]See especially studies on John of the Cross (listed in the Bibliography) by Burrows, Collings, Dicken, Doohan, Dubay, Hardy, Kavanaugh, Matthew, Muto, Payne, Tillyer, and Welch.

[6]On Elizabeth see especially H. Kane, *The Complete Works of Elizabeth of the Trinity*, Vol. 1, Washington, DC: Institute of Carmelite Studies, 1984, and A. E. Nash, *The Complete Works of Elizabeth of the Trinity*, Vol. 2, Washington, DC: Institute of Carmelite Studies, 1992.

[7]See studies on Elizabeth's teachings (listed in the Bibliography) by De Meester and Philipon, and my book, note 3 above.

found my heaven on earth, since heaven is God, and God is in my soul."[8]

We can, then, find heaven within, and it is here perhaps that we should especially seek it, since Jesus told us that the kingdom of God was within.

As she examines different passages of Scripture, Elizabeth sees the unfolding of God's plan of redemption for the human race. From the *Old Testament* and continuing through the *New Testament* the ways in which God relates to us and our response become ever more clear and explicit. Jesus, as Incarnate Word, fully reveals who the Father is. He also teaches us about the Holy Spirit who was sent to human beings at Pentecost. The Holy Spirit, as the "Spirit of truth" (John 16:13), abides within the human heart and teaches us the wishes of the life of God.[9]

While keeping this broad vision, Elizabeth also interpreted passages of Scripture on an "inner" level. Her question would be: What does this passage say of my soul? She then sees in the words of Scripture lessons for the soul and its nature and growth. In looking at passages of Scripture in this way, we do not restrict the meaning of the passage to any limited interpretation. Rather, Elizabeth teaches us to discern levels of meaning in various passages. She draws us to apply passages to an understanding of the soul. Passages then teach us more and more of the exquisite nature and destiny of our souls. What Elizabeth finds true of her own soul is true for us all.[10]

Let us look at one example. Psalm 19 begins: "The heavens declare the glory of God." Elizabeth is well aware that these words refer to the magnificent spectacle of God's creation. But she then applies this passage to what is happening in her own soul:[11]

---

[8]*Complete Works, Vol. 2, Letter 122,* p. 51.
[9]See Acts 5:30-32; 15:8-18; Romans 8:5-27; 1 Corinthians 6:19-20; 12:33; 2 Corinthians 1:21-22; Galatians 5:16-25; Ephesians 4:3-6; Titus 3:5-7.
[10]See especially her *Last Retreat* in *Complete Works, Vol. 1,* pp. 141-175.
[11]*Last Retreat,* p. 149.

This is what the heavens are telling: the glory of God. Since my soul is a heaven in which I live while awaiting the "heavenly Jerusalem," this heaven too must sing the glory of the Eternal, nothing but the glory of the Eternal.

We will apply Elizabeth's Carmelite perspective to various texts, showing how it draws us into a greater and deeper awareness of the divine presence within.

Direct Address

A powerful way to make a passage very immediate is to change references to persons into direct address. This technique must be applied with caution to ensure that the meaning of a passage is not altered or distorted. But often, correctly applied, this technique can bring us into the presence of God and Jesus in a new and vital way. As a brief example, let us take some verses of Psalm 91:14-16. (*Italic* type indicates changes made for direct address.)

Usual Translation[12]

Since he clings to me in love, I will free him;
protect him for he knows my name.
When he calls, I shall answer: "I am with you."
I will save him in distress and give him glory.

With length of life I will content him;
I shall let him see my saving power.

Direct Address

Since *I cling to you* in love, *you* will free *me*;
protect me for *I know your* name.
When *I call, you* shall answer: "I am with you."
You will save *me* in distress and give *me* glory.

With length of life *you* will content *me*;
You shall let *me* see *your* saving power.

---

[12]Taken from *Night Prayer* in *The Liturgy of the Hours,* New York: Catholic Book Publishing Co., 1975, Vol. 3, p. 1273.

Direct address helps us to understand what our role as Christians is. It brings us into the presence of God, removing all distance. God is not "there" but "right here." God we can address as "You." We encounter the love of this God in an intensely personal way. In the *Companion* we will use direct address in different passages where it can appropriately deepen our prayer.

Different Voices

As we read the various psalms in the *Hours*, we are often filled with amazement at how they may exactly express what we ourselves are feeling. If our hearts are singing with joy, the psalms of *Morning Prayer* may echo our gratitude to God and our praise for his goodness. If our hearts and minds are burdened with sorrow and distress, the psalms of the *Office of Readings* or *Evening Prayer* may echo our grief. If people in our lives harass or harm us, how well we find ourselves able to cry out to heaven in the words of the psalmist!

Ambrose well describes the wonderful nature of the psalms as sources of prayer for people in many different states:[13]

> In the Book of Psalms there is profit for all, with healing power for our salvation. There is instruction from history, teaching from the law, prediction from prophecy, chastisement from denunciation, persuasion from moral preaching. All who read it may find the cure for their own individual failings. All with eyes to see can discover in it a complete gymnasium for the soul, a stadium for all the virtues, equipped for every kind of exercise; it is for *all* to choose the kind *they judge* best to help *them* gain the prize.

First and foremost, therefore, the psalms can be our own voice, praying with earnest devotion to God. We

[13]*Explanation of the Psalms*, Ps. 1:4, in *Office of Readings* in *The Liturgy of the Hours* (as in note 12), Vol. 3, p. 343.

become one with the psalmist as the words express the thoughts and feelings of our souls. This possible identification helps to make the reading of the psalms meaningful. On a deeper level, it makes praying the psalms a personal encounter with God. Our feelings and circumstances are immediately present in the words we say.

The *Liturgy of the Hours,* however, is always much more than our own personal prayer. It is the prayer of the whole Church, uttered in many, many languages around the world. Thus, Ambrose says of the psalms:[14]

> Yes, a psalm is a blessing on the lips of the people, a hymn in praise of God, the assembly's homage, a general acclamation, a word that speaks for all, the voice of the Church, a confession of faith in song. It is the voice of complete assent, the joy of freedom, a cry of happiness, the echo of gladness.

Praying the psalms involves a "liturgy," a sacred act inspired by the Holy Spirit.[15] Thus, in a sense, one voice ascends to God from his Church. This is the voice of all the baptized rendering praise to God as is his due.

Yet, on a deeper level, there is another presence to be found in the psalms. The psalms proclaim the life and mission of Jesus. Once again Ambrose speaks clearly of this aspect of the psalms:[16]

> What am I to say of the grace of prophecy? We see that what others hinted at in riddles was promised openly and clearly to the psalmist alone: the Lord Jesus was to be born of *David's* seed, according to the word of the Lord, *I will place upon your throne one who is the fruit of your flesh.*

---

[14]*Explanation of the Psalms,* Ps. 1:9 (as in note 12), Vol. 3, p. 347.

[15]On this meaning of "liturgy" see H. M. Roguet, OP, *The Liturgy of the Hours,* trans. P. Coughlan and P. Purdue, Collegeville, MN: Liturgical Press, 1971, pp. 84-88.

[16]*Explanation of the Psalms,* Ps. 1:7-8 (as in note 12), Vol. 3, p. 344.

In the psalms, then, not only is Jesus born for us, he also undergoes his saving passion in his body, he lies in death, he rises again, he ascends into heaven, he sits at the right hand of the Father. What no one would have dared to say was foretold by the psalmist alone, and afterward proclaimed by the Lord himself in the Gospel.

Yet in the psalms we can go a step deeper. We must not only learn about Jesus but also hear his voice in prayer. But which Jesus is this? Jesus, we know, is now reigning in heaven in the presence of his Father, the angels, and all the saints. Which Jesus would be praying in the psalms? This Jesus is he who is present in the souls of all the faithful, in your soul and my soul.

This voice of Jesus is present in the *Hours*; it is a voice that prays to the Father.[17] Always the Church identifies with Jesus as he obeys the Father and offers him praise. In the *Hours* this activity of Jesus appears to be particularly evident. If we remember that it is Jesus, present within our souls, who is praying, we can partake in the *Hours* in a profoundly spiritual way. This perspective helps us to move beyond ourselves into a new level of consciousness.

What happens if we listen for the voice of Jesus? Psalms take on a new richness and depth not perceived before. We are constantly drawn out of our own limited experience into a deeper way of praying. For example, on some occasions, we may encounter a psalm full of sorrow although we, at that moment, are not experiencing grief. If we listen for the voice of Jesus, we can forget ourselves and try to see things from his point of view. So too with psalms expressing joy, wonder, delight, we can see the experiences they describe as those of Jesus. When the psalmist cries out in pain or

[17]Roguet, pp. 87-88.

in anguish over the treatment received from enemies, we can move out of our own lives and ponder deeply the sufferings of Jesus. As Christians, we are called to love Jesus and, by loving him, to be transformed into him:

> Although you have not seen him, you love him; and even though you do not see him now yet believe in him, you rejoice with an indescribable and glorious joy, as you attain the goal of [your] faith, the salvation of your souls (1 Peter 1:8).

> He has bestowed on us the precious and very great promises, so that through them you may come to share in the divine nature (2 Peter 1:4).

The more we hear the voice of Jesus in the psalms, the more we will come to understand who he is and what we are called to be.

In terms of voices, therefore, the *Hours* may be our own voice, the voice of the Church, or the voice of Jesus. The possibility of these different voices allows us to enter in an individual yet universal way into the *Hours*. It also, in particular, allows us to share in the prayer that Jesus makes to the Father. We take part in the "liturgy," the holy act by which God is praised.[18] The psalms reveal the whole range of human experience in which Jesus shared. The *Hours* make this sharing present now in our time. The voice of Jesus sanctifies all that human beings feel and suffer and offers all to the Father. The more we pray the *Hours*, the more our voice and the voice of the Church become the voice of Jesus. We enter ever more deeply into the life of prayer. We move from "saying" the *Hours* ourselves to "praying" the *Hours* ourselves and then, at a deeper level, to "praying" the *Hours* with Jesus, in close identity with his Church.

---

[18]Roguet, pp. 87-91.

Structure of the *Companion*

1. The *Companion* will offer a commentary on the psalms, canticles, and readings of *Morning* and *Evening Prayer* of the 4-week cycle.

2. The *Companion* will discuss in detail the *Canticle of Zechariah* and *Canticle of Mary* since they form a part of every *Morning* and *Evening Prayer.*

3. The *Companion* will include the antiphons when discussion of them seems appropriate. In some cases these antiphons simply summarize the content of the psalms or canticle. In other cases they add interesting thematic highlights to these selections.

4. When appropriate, the *Companion* will refer to the sentences (printed in *italics*) chosen from Scripture or the Fathers of the Church that precede each psalm. These sentences place the psalms in a Christian context, relating them to the new revelation of Christ.

Language in the *Companion*

1. The texts for the psalms, canticles, and readings will be taken from the *Liturgy of the Hours* (New York: Catholic Book Publishing Co., 1975).

2. Two other editions have been consulted, as indicated in the bibliography. These are the *People's Companion to the Breviary,* which uses inclusive language, and *Psalms: Morning and Evening,* which presents new, poetic translations of the psalms.

3. Texts in the edition of the *Liturgy of the Hours* we are using do not yet use inclusive language, but care will be taken in the *Companion* to speak inclusively, wherever it is appropriate.

4. In the commentaries on different texts, the *Companion* will use the pronouns "he," "his," "him"

for "God" in order to allow the text to flow easily along. The use of these pronouns does not ascribe gender to God who is pure spirit.

5. In our discussion of the *Liturgy of the Hours*, we will use the shortened form of *"Hours"* as we discuss *Morning* and *Evening Prayer.* Sometimes we will call *Morning* and *Evening Prayer* "offices," recalling their origins as "duties" related to certain times of the day.

Instructions for Using This *Companion*

The following are suggestions for use of this Companion as one says the *Liturgy of the Hours.*

1. First, read through the whole of either *Morning* or *Evening Prayer* in the *Liturgy of the Hours.*

2. Quietly reflect on which of the following spoke most to your heart and soul: a psalm, the canticle, or the reading.

3. Take up the *Companion* and read the commentary on that particular selection.

4. Lay the *Companion* aside and for a few minutes listen deep within to what God is saying to your heart.

5. In terms of time, it may be that only one *Hour* can be said each day. This is fine! Better to give a half hour to "praying" one *Hour* well than the same time to "saying" several *Hours* with little inner attention.

6. As you say *Morning* or *Evening Prayer* over a period of time, gradually read different selections from the *Companion* until all have been covered.

7. Once a week choose the *Canticle of Zechariah* and/or the *Canticle of Mary* as your selection for prayer. Read the *Companion*. Spend a few minutes in silent reflection on these passages. Those Gospel canticles, read every day, will become rich sources for reflection and spiritual growth.

1.

Week I: Morning and Evening Prayer

*We shall see the beauty of your face
in the splendor of goodness.*

I: Morning Prayer

Sunday

Sunday, Week I, Morning Prayer we can describe as of vital interest. The two psalms and canticle begin our month of praise. We discover too that for all major feasts these portions are read even though the rest of the office may be different. Furthermore, only the selections of *Morning Prayer* of *Sunday, Week I,* are used on all feasts, not those of *Evening Prayer I* or *II.* How important, then, must these selections be! What psalms and canticle has the Church judged to express most fittingly the praise and reverence due to God on every joyous feast?

Psalm 63:2-9

This psalm uses direct address. How close we feel to God's presence in talking to him directly. And yet, at first, he is a presence that we seek and seem not to find. Then we encounter his love filling our being. Our days, yes, and our nights are enriched by his love. This psalm, therefore, expresses the experience of every person seeking God. We search for, we long after, we suffer the lack of God. When he is found, our joy knows no bounds. The Church calls on us to remember this experience every Sunday of *Week I* and every feast day throughout the year.

We can hear three voices in this psalm: our own, that of the whole Church, and that of Jesus dwelling within our souls. In our own voice we express our intense longing for God. On one level, we can look outward for this God, searching the heavens, seeking through the universe for his presence. To us, sometimes, he may seem close, but now, sadly, he seems far away. The psalmist suggests that God is distant. We are like a desert, "a dry, weary land without water." But God lives! He has his holy place; he is radiant with glory.

As we read this first stanza our perspective may also be Carmelite. The God we look for, the God we long for, is in the center of our souls. There is his "sanctuary"; there is his glory. But we have not yet found him. We are thirsting for his presence. We fix our inner gaze on him.

Stanza one describes how empty and barren we are without God. Stanza two tells us what happens when God floods our souls with his presence. The joy, the vitality, that we may feel within as life flows through our bodies is wonderful. But God's love exceeds "life" in great measure. Best to be filled with this love! When we are, something so amazing happens within that our whole inner being is transformed. Praise wells up inside us.

Our lips pour forth this praise. We become aware of God's presence in a way that will last our whole life. We are empowered by God so that it is in his "name," in his strength and vigor, that we act. We "lift up" our hands. Our whole being is suffused with divine grace just as though our soul were at a "banquet." It is "with joy" that praise pours from our lips.

Stanza three describes how pervasive God's love can be. It is not only during the day that his presence transforms our lives. At night we think of God. We recall all the ways in which he has helped us. We realize one important truth: abiding in the divine presence brings safety. There we can rejoice. We are in a reciprocal relationship. Our soul "clings" to God, and God holds us "fast."

In the Carmelite view, this God acts from within our being. When we do not find him, we long for him intensely. When he is there, our whole being is transformed from within by his presence. He fills our mouths with praise. He empowers our actions. He gives us all inner riches. Through the night he remains an abiding presence. Inwardly, we cling to him, and he "holds" us firmly. God moves from the deep center of our hearts and makes himself known. The result is endless praise and joy.

In this psalm too we can hear the voice of Jesus as he dwells in our souls. He longs for the Father and looks for him. When he is filled with the Father's love, he praises, blesses, rejoices. He stays with the Father at all times, at night remembering, musing, clinging, ever held "fast." This Jesus is within us, loving us and praying for us. We can feel compassion for him as he shares our lives with us. When he is longing for God, our hearts weep for him. When he feels the presence of his Father, we rejoice at his joy. We come to share deeply in the life of Jesus. We realize that he is sharing equally in our spiritual life.

Canticle: Daniel 3:57-88, 56

This lovely canticle, preserved in the Septuagint, draws our hearts and minds to ponder the whole expanse of the universe. This song, sung by Hananiah, Azariah, and Mishael in the fiery furnace, proclaims their staunch and immovable faith in God. In the furnace where the flames did not sear nor the heat destroy, their joy knew no bounds. God kept them safe and did not leave them alone. The king who had cast them into the furnace, Nebuchadnezzar, saw with astonishment that a fourth presence was walking with the three young men (Daniel 3:24). In the furnace, they turn their eyes outward and call on all of nature to praise and bless the Lord.

Knowing the context of this canticle, we see the Church teaching us a profound lesson, one that we will recall on every Sunday of *Week I* and on every feast day of the year. The three young men were willing to die for their faith. With courage, they chose death and were cast into the raging flames. God did not fail them! He turned an experience of terror and horror into a victory. Flames and heat became the sweetness of God's presence in a "dew-laden breeze" (Daniel 3:50). So we, when faced with the challenges of life in whatever form they come, have here a model of behavior. In the face of attack from without, illness, pain, loss of loved ones, and all sorrow, we can be sure that God is faithful. He will be with us as a consoling presence. He will give us cause to burst forth into a song of praise. We will want all creation to know of his goodness. We will call on all God's creatures to bless him.

In this canticle, we can discern all three of our "voices." This call for praise is my call. In my personal life I can think of situations where God blessed me, and I would want the whole universe to bless him in turn for his goodness. This call for praise is that of the Church as a whole. How the universal Church can speak of the faithfulness and goodness of God! All we creatures receive our existence from God. We human beings owe our redemption to God and also our hopes for heaven. God creates, sustains, redeems, and sanctifies us moment by moment. Surely we wish the whole of creation to bless this God of ours.

The third voice is that of Jesus. The canticle can be truly his. Begotten of the Father and sent into our world, Jesus faced the horror of the crucifixion. He was not saved from death as the three young men were. Instead, becoming "sin" for us (2 Corinthians 5:21), he destroyed death itself with his triumphant return to life on this very day of resurrection that we are celebrating. Now, with the Father and also living in our souls, he can utter this canticle of triumph and joy. Yes, this is the song of Jesus!

In a special way this canticle can be the song of Jesus for the Father. We hear of Jesus:

He was in the world,
and the world came to be through him.

(John 1:10)

Paul tells us also of Jesus:

He is the image of the invisible God,
the firstborn of all creation.
For in him were created all things in heaven and
earth,
the visible and the invisible,
whether thrones or dominions or principalities or
powers;
all things were created through him and for him.

(Colossians 1:15-16)

The Father created his universe through his Word, Jesus. How fitting to hear in this canticle the call of Jesus for all his creation to praise and glorify the Father!

Can we look at this canticle from a Carmelite perspective? The canticle calls on all the natural phenomena in the universe to respond with joy to the presence of God. In a similar vein we might look within and take into consideration all the faculties that God has given us: intellect, imagination, memory, understanding, and especially our free will. We may wish to call upon these gifts to praise God. Most of all, we may center our will in our hearts and, like Hananiah, Azariah, and Mishael, who are "humble of heart," praise God in complete adoration. Inwardly, therefore, we can strive to love the Lord, our God, "with all *our* heart, and with all *our* souls, and with all *our* strength" (Deuteronomy 6:5), matching the praise that all creation pours forth.

Psalm 149

In this third psalm of *Morning Prayer* the call is for the human being to praise God. It thus continues the call for praise found in the canticle from Daniel. In this canticle all creation is summoned to bless God with the final verses calling upon human beings to do the same. Psalm 149 teaches us *how* we are to praise: we are to sing a "new song." This exhortation is in accord with the nature of our spiritual journey. The past is gone; the present we can spend with God. The future is yet unreal but, if we get the present right, the future will be also right. Always, ever, from our souls a new song is to arise. We are different each day. There is always a new list of blessings which can form the substance of our song and can be the foundation of our gratitude.

Stanza one asks us to sing. Stanza two gives two reasons for this singing. First, God is delighted with us. What a wonderfully positive picture of God this is! We know that God loves us, but this description suggests that God likes our company, our actions, our personalities. Second, we wish to sing because, as we recognize our needs, as we happily call ourselves "poor" in relation to all inner righteousness, as we perceive how much grace we lack, we discover that God gives us "salvation." This gift becomes our "glory." With it we can "shout for joy" and "take our rest."

In those two stanzas that summon us to "sing a new song" with joy, dancing, and music, we can discern two voices. First, our own that we are to raise in song, and second, the voice of the Church as it offers new praise to God. The Church is the new Israel and new Zion crowned with salvation and giving delight to God.

What, however, are we to make of the end of the second stanza and the final stanza with their references to punishment inflicted with a "two-edged sword"? We are told that to give punishment to "nations," "peoples," "kings," and "nobles" is an honor for God's "faithful." Clearly none of us is going to perform this action in a literal way. With these lines the Carmelite perspective becomes valuable.

Looking at the psalm as a whole from this perspective we see a call to us, within our souls, to "sing a new song," to "rejoice" and "exult." We see our souls as "poor" but crowned with "salvation." It is within that we will direct our powers of punishment. All in us that can be a source of sin, pride, or self-enhancement we can curb and restrain. Our faith makes it possible for us to discern what needs to be checked or rejected within. We will do so gladly and consider it an honor because such a course of action makes us "poor" in self and it is the poor that receive salvation.

From the Carmelite perspective, the "new song" comes from within. The whole person is to rejoice, dance, and sing because God "takes delight" in us and "crowns" us with "salvation." This is the essential truth of Christianity and explains why this song is appropriate for *Sunday Week I* and for all great feasts. Those who are saved are people who have chosen the "narrow gate" and the "constricted . . . road that leads to life" (Matthew 7:13). Constantly curbing all that is alien to the increase of grace, souls find that they can "rejoice in their glory, shout for joy and take their rest."

Reading: Revelation 7:10,12

The selection is brief but contains the essence of our position as Christians. We have been saved by the will of God. Jesus became the Lamb sacrificed for us. Everything that we can imagine human beings giving to God and everything that we imagine God being are now described: "Praise and glory, wisdom and thanksgiving and honor, power and might." To such a situation we add: "So be it! Amen!"

Monday

Psalm 5:2-10, 12-13

Our week begins and we are aware of how long it may be. In this psalm we speak in our voice and in the voice of the Church, crying out for help. We recognize our great need for God. To him we send up the "groaning" and "sound" of cries. We address him directly. The next stanza delightfully refers to the time of our prayer: "in the morning" God hears us; "in the morning" we offer prayer. Our attitude is to keep our eyes on God: we watch and we wait. The psalm then speaks further to God, describing his nature. We perceive evil in our world, but we affirm that God does not love evil. The sinner and boastful person does not have a place in his presence. Evil, lies, deceit—these human actions we must shun. But we, we are blessed to be able to enter the house of God, and it is love that has drawn us there. With awe we acknowledge God's presence.

In the next stanza we turn our attention to God asking for what we need. It is he who is to lead us; we are to follow. It is he who makes his way clear to us. We are surrounded in our world by people who do not believe. These people may do what we heard above: lie, deceive, plan evil. We, however, put ourselves under the protection of God and there we rejoice and are glad. God shelters us; our love is for him. Blessings that fall on the just person come from the Lord. If we are just, we find God's favor surrounding us and protecting us as though we were behind a "shield."

If we adopt the Carmelite perspective, we can say this psalm, directing our gaze inward to God dwelling in our souls. We call on God within and want him to hear our cries. "In the morning" we watch and wait for this Divine Guest. And who must we be who call on him within? We must reject in our own natures all evil:

our tendencies to boast, to lie, to deceive, to be violent.

It is God's love that draws us inward to our "temple," that is, to the core of our soul where God dwells. We are astounded at his generosity and filled with awe. We ask God to lead us. We have enemies within, namely our sinful tendencies. We need to learn what God's way might be. God will protect us; he shelters us; he surrounds us with favor, all from within. How we rejoice to find that this is so! We are truly those who love God's name.

In this psalm too we can hear the voice of Jesus crying out as he dwells in our hearts. We hear him calling out to the Father, praying in the morning, watching and waiting for the response of the Father. Jesus knows that the Father will resist and punish sinners. He himself adores the Father, ever doing his will. The sinfulness of each one of us hinders the growth and activity in our hearts, but the Father guards Jesus. He shelters and surrounds him within. As we say the psalm with Jesus' voice, our love for him grows. We long to help him as he redeems us and the world. We try to let his voice in us be one of joy as he celebrates our striving to be just. We attempt to keep him from "groaning" and, instead, to allow his morning prayer to be a song of rejoicing.

Canticle: 1 Chronicles 29:10-13

In the canticle we hear three voices: ours, the Church's, and that of Jesus. All unite in one wondrous hymn of praise for the Father. Ah, what a wondrous God we have! All "grandeur and power, majesty, splendor, and glory" are his. The whole universe belongs to him. From him all blessings come. Our response to who God is: gratitude and praise.

From the Carmelite perspective we hear of God ruling over all things and, in particular, our souls. We are astonished at the nature of this God who is willing to dwell at the center of our souls. Our whole being—body, soul, spirit—belongs to him. All the gifts, talents, and strengths we possess are from him. Our response before this Divine Guest is to give thanks and to praise.

Psalm 29

In this psalm we are called on to recognize the "glory and power" of God. We fix our eyes on the court of the Father in heaven. We see the effects of his "voice" on the sea and the land. It is as if we are in the midst of a mighty storm that stirs up the waters, shatters trees, and strips the forest. This storm is filled with lightning and thunder. Yet God is not in the storm but above it, reigning and honored by his court. It is this God who will strengthen us and give us peace. How could we fear with such a king? He will be with us as we begin our week of labor.

Reading: 2 Thessalonians 3:10b-13

In this reading we learn what our attitude to work should be. We are quietly "to earn" our food. We must find a constant joy in doing "what is right."

Tuesday

Psalm 24

In this psalm we look at God and then at the type of person who can worthily approach him. If we begin the psalm with direct address, we are drawn quickly into the presence of God:

Yours, Lord, is the earth and its fullness,
the world and all its peoples.
It is you who set it on the seas;
on the waters you made it firm.

Then we ask: Who shall come into the presence of God? We are to be virtuous and honest in actions and pure of heart. We are not to desire "worthless things." We do not "deceive" our neighbor. If we look carefully at this description, we see a picture of the whole person. Outwardly and inwardly we are to strive for goodness and purity. Our desires are to be carefully directed. To our neighbor we show honesty.

If we aim to be such a person, God will bless us. The remainder of the psalm describes a procession of pilgrims into the temple of God. The pilgrims utter the description of God while the questions come from within the temple. For us, however, the call is for God to enter our lives, richly, fully. God is "mighty," "valiant," and "king of glory." We long for his presence.

From a Carmelite perspective, this psalm presents a wonderful message. The whole of our being belongs to God, and he dwells as a guest in the center of our souls. How shall we come into his presence? First, our actions should be virtuous, our desires on worthy things, our approach to our neighbor, honest. But, perhaps most importantly, our heart is to be pure. Jesus has told us: "Blessed are the clean of heart, for they will see God" (Matthew 5:8).

The blessing that we shall receive is "the face of the God of Jacob." But we will need to make room for God. We make room in our souls, emptying out all that is not of God and letting the "king of glory" dwell therein. We invite God to dwell fully in our souls. We invite God to enter his whole temple, all of our being. As the Lord fills the whole universe, he will likewise fill our whole being. But this will happen, specifically at our invitation, only if we strive to "stand in his holy place."

We may present an image of our making ourselves ready, actively choosing virtue, zealously emptying ourselves of what is unworthy. We come gently, quietly into God's presence within our souls. Once there, we may earnestly desire that this wondrous God fill our whole being with his holy presence. Yes, he is ours and we are entirely his.

Canticle: Tobit 13:1-8

In this canticle we can hear two voices, our own and that of the Church. All of us and the Church as a whole often find ourselves feeling like "aliens" in the world. But here we have a mission, to proclaim God's love, and here we will still find the presence of God. We may suffer in this setting but from this too we can learn.

How is it that God acts? If we use direct address in this psalm, we see clearly something of his activity.

Blessed are you, God, who *live* forever,
because *your* kingdom lasts for all ages.

For *you scourge* and then *have* mercy;
you cast down to the depths of the nether world,
and *you bring* up from the great abyss.
No one can escape *your* hand.

We learn that God punishes and shows compassion. We are then called on to praise this great God (3-4). Once again we hear of his punishment and mercy (5-8).

The psalm tells us that our own behavior determines our treatment. God hides "his face" when we turn from him. When we turn back to him "with all *our* heart," he will be there for us. We should praise this wondrous God!

When we feel we are among aliens, our task is to praise God and reveal his "power and majesty" to those who may not believe in him. My wish for them is what I have found for myself. If we do "what is right" before God, he will show us favor and mercy.

This canticle helps us to approach the day before us. The challenge for us is to keep turning to God "with all *our* heart." We may turn away under the pressure of distractions, stress, or hardships. But, if we do, we will lose God's presence. Then we may not do what is right and should not be surprised if we face punishment. But mercy is ever there, awaiting our return. God is there, waiting to bless us. As often as we turn to him during the day, we will find him. And so, in light of this knowledge, we praise God and call on all to do likewise.

Psalm 33

This psalm picks up the theme of the canticle. We find a description of God, his control of nature and the nations, and we hear how we should respond. The voice of the psalm may be ours or the Church's as it presents a description of who God is and how human beings are related to him.

As we approach God our one response is to be joy. All our skill and energies are to be used in praise of God. Why? Because God is faithful; he "fills the earth with his love." We then look at the universe God has made: heavens, stars, oceans, seas, earth. God created all of these and sustains them. We then should revere him.

With regard to human beings, God's will is supreme. Nations may make plans, but these God may frustrate. So too in the case of our personal plans, God's will may be different. What we can be sure of is that God's "designs" will be fulfilled and they last from "age to age."

The psalmist then presents a picture of reality. Those who honor God are his people: happiness is theirs. God lovingly regards the universe he has made. His activity is to shape our "hearts" and consider our "deeds." Human strength alone is of no avail; neither is any creature in which we might trust. It is God who will rescue us from danger, whether famine or death.

How should we human beings act? We are to wait for the Lord and to trust in him. We will find that he is "our help and our shield." It is in him that our hearts are to find joy. Our relationship will be a reciprocal one: we place all hope in God while he pours love into us.

From the Carmelite perspective we may see very clearly how we are to relate to God within our souls. The psalm speaks much of the state of our "hearts" at the center of which we believe that God dwells. First, if we look at the role of human beings within the psalm, we see that with "loyal hearts" we are to praise God with joy. We recognize God's power over us as creatures: he is shaping our hearts. We are warned not to make plans apart from God but to see his "designs." We learn not to trust our own strength or that of other creatures. Rescue will come only from God. We are to wait for the Lord and to trust in him as "our help and our shield," present within our very beings. In this Divine Guest we place all our hope.

Second, if we look at God's activity in the psalm, we see how he loves his people. This love is described as coming from without, suffusing the universe and working its purposes. But we can also see it as coming from within. It fills our being. It controls our actions if we yield to it. It shapes our hearts, transforming us with its presence. We are "to hope" in this love and it will not fail us. Within we will find the Lord as "our help and our shield." We pray that his love will suffuse our whole being, and our hope is that this will occur. When it does, "our hearts find joy."

This psalm presents a universal view of God. But we can see in it also a particular view of God's work in each soul. As we are loved and cared for from within, we rejoice with even greater joy to realize that God fills the universe in a similar way. The Carmelite perspective helps us to see how we are individually loved. It increases our love for all of God's creation that he is guiding, protecting, and rescuing.

Reading: Romans 13:11b, 12-13a

In this brief passage we are called on to begin our day in a wakeful state. We are to be filled with light, acting with honor and integrity. Inwardly we are to mirror the daylight in which we move. Clearly we are to radiate God's life within us. Psalm 33 has shown us how God dwells within, loving, guiding, and saving us. Now we are to let that inner life of light shine forth for others.

Wednesday

Psalm 36

In this psalm our eyes turn in two directions. First, we look at the person who is a sinner. We know full well that we could be, and may have been, this individual. The psalmist presents a penetrating and clear analysis of what happens when we sin. The temptation comes at a deep level. The "depths of *the* heart" are its target. The heart could have a defense: "fear of God." If this is lacking, we can begin to think incorrectly. We fail to realize our guilt. Actions that are wrong seem to be acceptable. Speech becomes full of deceit. The mind loses all wisdom.

Our behavior becomes worse and worse. We use our minds to plan evil. We begin to walk in evil ways, and, even worse, we begin to cling to evil. It seems very attractive to us.

Second, the psalm turns our attention to God. In gazing at who God is, we join those who have "fear of God." And what do we see? Many features that remove our fears of sinners and draw us to avoid sin ourselves. God loves us with a love that "reaches to heaven." We address God directly and state this about his love. In this type of address how close we feel to God! We say to God: "your truth [reaches] to the skies." "Your justice" is like a mighty, tall mountain. "Your judgments" are as profound as the depths of the ocean. In the next verse we say: "you give protection." You provide "refuge" for human beings. The image of the "wings," found frequently in Scripture (see also Psalm 57:1; 63:7; 91:4), is that of God overshadowing the Ark with the winged cherubim. What a shelter for us do we find in this image!

In these two stanzas we thus encounter the following characteristics of God: love, truth, justice, judgments, protection, and refuge. It is in him that we put our trust. If we meet sinners in our lives, we are not afraid. If we are tempted to sin, we can remember who God is and alter our behavior. In the next stanza we hear how fortunate those who love God are. Again, in direct address we speak of feasting on "the riches of your house" and drinking from "the stream of your delight." We then sum up who God is for us: "in you is the source of life and in your light we see light." Thus our very "life" comes from God; our perception of "light" comes from him. The "light" helps us to live virtuous lives.

We then make a prayer for God's favor on those who hold him in awe. We want God's love; we long for his justice. As we look again on "evil-doers" we ask for God's protection. The psalm ends with a warning to those who do evil, both others and ourselves: a fall, from which recovery is impossible, awaits such people.

This psalm directs our attention first to something negative, the nature of sin and its effects, second to God and his wondrous qualities, and, finally, back to sin and its inevitable defeat. Abiding in God's love, we are safe, we feast, we are filled with life and light. We have no fear because God is love, truth, and justice, all boundless and all ours.

Canticle: Judith 16:2-3a, 13-15

In these lines we encounter the song of triumph as Judith rejoices in overcoming her enemies. She calls on her companions to praise God exuberantly. Then, turning to direct address, she speaks to God of his wondrous nature: "great," "glorious," "wonderful in power," "unsurpassable." All creation should praise God since our existence depends on him. "You spoke," "you sent forth your spirit," and all creation appeared. No person, nothing in nature can resist God. For those who stand in awe of God, who "fear" him, one experience is crucial: God is "merciful."

Just as in Psalm 36, we address God directly in this canticle and stand in awe of who he is. We acclaim his power and strength. Most of all, we are grateful for his mercy.

Psalm 47

In this psalm, as in the other two texts, we approach our day with joy. God is a great king who brings us victory because he loves us. Our acknowledgment of God's kingship over all is accompanied by "shouts of joy" and "trumpet" blasts. Our whole response is to be one of praise. God's reign extends over the nations and the earth. All princes and rulers are subordinate to him.

From the Carmelite point of view we can envision this majestic reign of God as occurring within our souls. The "earth" he governs is our body. The enemies he overcomes are our own evil tendencies. He loves us and fills us with glory, radiating from within. We wish to honor God who is enshrined in our hearts. We can ask him to take his throne within with "trumpet" blasts and "shouts of joy" and "praise." This mighty king of the universe dwells within our souls. What can our response be except delight and adoration?

Reading: Tobit 4:15a, 16a, 18a, and 19

In these lines Tobit gives advice to his son Tobiah on how to live with integrity and honor. We are never to do to others what we would not wish done to us. Our eyes are to be compassionate, feeding the hungry, clothing the naked. When we need advice, it is to the wise person we are to go. Always, and most importantly, we are to abide in God's presence, blessing him for who he is, praying for his guidance, and asking him to make our actions successful.

Truly these verses sum up the behavior of the person striving to live a life of love. God is to be the center of our lives as we acknowledge who he is and ask for his assistance. To our neighbor we show honor equal to that which we accord ourselves: we do not do what we dislike to have done to us. We seek out the wise; we help the needy.

Thursday

Psalm 57

In this psalm we can hear our own voice and that of the Church. We are in great distress, crying aloud to God for help. We have taken refuge in God; we have hidden in the "shadow of [his] wings." We ask for his mercy, hoping that he will protect and keep us from harm. It is to God, ever helpful, that we pray. His most valuable gifts are "truth" and "love."

As we gaze on our circumstances, we feel as though we are amid "lions" ready to devour us. People attack us with weapons of speech. What we need is God! These enemies have laid snares for us but, to our astonishment, were caught in their own devices. Surely God came to our aid! Our joy is very great: we want all creation to awake and learn of our experience. God did send his "love" and "truth." These are so great that they fill all the heavens. We wish God to have full power, he "above the heavens," and his glory shining "on earth."

In this psalm we can hear also the voice of Jesus crying out during his sufferings. For our sake he became an atonement for our sins, a sacrifice for all our faults.

His attackers fiercely pursued him. On the cross, his
"soul was bowed down" but inwardly he clung to God.
"Truth" and "love" prevailed, and on the third day Jesus
rose from the dead. Then his cry was one of joy; then he
eagerly wanted the dawn to awake, to recognize what
the Father had done. God's "love reaches to the heavens," his "truth to the skies." Jesus is Lord: God's
"glory" has shone on the earth.

Canticle: Jeremiah 31:10-14

For us Christians this canticle describes our joy at
the resurrection of Jesus. Our blessings are indescrib-
ably wonderful. God has fulfilled the prophecy that he
made to Jeremiah. If we use direct address as we read
this description of a happy celebration, we perceive
more exactly what God has done for us.

> *You* who scattered Israel, now *gather us* together,
> *you guard us* as a shepherd his flock.
> *You, Lord,* shall ransom Jacob,
> *you* shall redeem *us* from the hand of our conqueror.
> Shouting, *we* shall mount the heights of Zion,
> *we* shall come streaming to the Lord's blessings. . . .
> *We ourselves* shall be like watered gardens,
> never again shall *we* languish.
> Then the virgins shall make merry and dance,
> and young men and old as well.
> I will turn *your* mourning into joy,
> I will console and gladden *you* after *your* sorrows.
> I will lavish choice portions upon the priests,
> and my people shall be filled with my blessings,
> says the Lord.

From a Carmelite perspective, we perceive God's
action in our souls. We come to the center of our hearts
and there we encounter many, many blessings of God:
his very presence. We are "like watered gardens" with-

in. In his presence "never again shall [we] languish." We may have grieved and felt sorrow, but now we feel immense joy.

Psalm 48

This psalm presents a picture of "Mount Zion" and Jerusalem: these are the places where God has chosen to dwell. On one level we can share the sense of wonder and joy that the psalmist feels in describing this "city" of God. Of all the earth Mount Zion is joy. God is the "stronghold" of Jerusalem. Its very aspect fills its enemies with fear. God destroys those who would attack it. There will never be need of fear for Jerusalem because "God upholds" it always. Within God's temple, we think about how he loves us. We know too that his power extends over the whole earth. Since this is so, we need not be afraid. We are filled with joy because God is just. As we gaze on God's temple, we are filled with awe and wonder at God. He remains ever the same and always leads us.

On a second level we can think of ourselves as temples of the Holy Spirit. It is in our hearts that God lives: "in the midst of [our] citadels." God is our stronghold. Within ourselves we recognize evil tendencies that attack us, but these seem to disappear before the light of God. God is our support. He fills us with his love and our whole being praises him. This God is a God of justice. We are amazed that God has made us his dwelling place. From within he leads us. We want to proclaim his truth to all.

Reading: Isaiah 66:1-2

In this reading God tells us that he created the whole universe, the heavens and the earth. We human beings could never make a place for God to rest in. But there is something of which God approves: the humble person. We learn that there is a "kind of house" that we can make for God: a lowly heart filled with awe of God. We cannot build him anything exterior to ourselves, but, in our own being, we can become what delights him.

Friday

Psalm 51

Every Friday the *Liturgy of the Hours* begins *Morning Prayer* with Psalm 51. Friday is the day in which we recall in particular the passion of Jesus. How often in the psalms of the different hours we can hear his voice. How fitting also to begin Friday with this Psalm 51, a cry of the sinner for God's mercy. In this psalm we recognize that we have done wrong in God's sight. We trust in his mercy and, therefore, we confess with confidence the true state of our souls. The first three stanzas give a specific picture of the state of the human soul. We need God's mercy and compassion. God can wash and cleanse us. We recognize that all sin has been committed against God. His judgment is based on truth and is always justified. We realize that we have free will and that we have sinned, using this free will in a negative way.

One of the most powerful features of this psalm is the direct address that it uses. In these stanzas I talk directly to God. Thus I recognize my sinfulness and ask for mercy. God wants me to be a person of truth and to recognize in my heart my sinfulness. What I wish to be taught is "wisdom": to see myself as I am, and God as he is, especially in his mercy. The wonder of God is that he can "purify" and "wash" me. When he removes my sense of guilt, I can rejoice. Then inwardly I "revive." What I long for most is a "pure heart" and a "steadfast spirit." What I fear most is to be "cast" from the presence of God or deprived of his "spirit": I long to stay close to the One who can heal, cleanse, and purify my soul.

As the psalm continues I begin to see the effects of God's presence in my heart. I ask for the "joy" of God's help and a "spirit of fervor." God will purify my heart and then fill me with a zeal for what is true, especially for his mercy. Thus filled, I will be able to draw others to him. My "tongue" will speak of God's "goodness." Under the influence of grace I will utter "praise." I recognize what God values: not sacrifice and not burnt offering. Instead, I offer a different kind of "sacrifice," a "contrite spirit."

The final stanza asks God to be kind to all of Zion and to "rebuild the walls of Jerusalem." When this happens, the people, purified within, will carry out the ceremonies in the temple in an acceptable way.

From the Christian point of view, this psalm brings us very close to Jesus. As we offer our prayers to God the Father, we know that forgiveness comes to us through the sacrifice of Jesus on the cross. He has made us "whiter than snow." He has made it possible for us to have a "pure heart." For us, the reference to the "holy spirit" takes on a deep meaning: we have received the Spirit of Jesus, the Holy Spirit, at confirmation. As we rejoice in the mercy that God the Father has bestowed on us in Jesus, we are eager to draw others to him. We have learned to have "a humbled, contrite heart," transformed by the grace that Jesus won for us. In the final stanza we can also understand the lines in a Christian sense. At each Mass Jesus is the "lawful sacrifice" who offers himself for our salvation. Earnestly we desire to be present, cleansed, forgiven, rejoicing.

Canticle: Isaiah 45:15-25

In this canticle we learn about God, who he is, what he has done, and what the future will hold. He is a God for all nations, and his plan of salvation is for all. As Christians, we believe strongly that this is so, convinced that acceptance of the sacrifice of Jesus will bring us grace and salvation. As we read this canticle in a Christian context, we encounter the wide-ranging plan of God, conceived of from the beginning and gradually unfolding as time passes.

Our God, the God of Israel, is a "hidden God." As pure spirit, no image can represent him. As savior of the universe, he can easily punish those who oppose him. God's nature is to be a saving God, and we can rejoice that we are "saved forever."

In the canticle we then hear God speak. This God made the universe and made it to be lived in. God tells us that he has made himself known in the past. He is a God of justice and right. He is a God who has "announced . . . from the beginning" what was to be. He "foretold it from of old." Just as he has done in the past, we can expect that he will do in the present and the future. Who is God? A "just and saving God."

God calls on all people: "turn to me and be safe." Then God utters a "just decree" and an "unalterable word." To him all knees will bend; by him all tongues will swear, recognizing that God alone is just. Even those who oppose him will come showing homage. All people of faith will find "vindication and . . . glory."

In a Christian context we believe that God has saved the world. Paul picks up the image of the "bending knee" in saying of Jesus (Philippians 2:10-11):

At the name of Jesus
every knee should bend,
of those in heaven and on earth and under the earth,
and every tongue confess that
Jesus Christ is Lord,
to the glory of God the Father.

We have seen God's "just deeds and power," especially when he raised Jesus from the dead. Turning to God the

Father with faith in Jesus, we find that we are "safe." Now we can pass our lives in this universe made by God "to be lived in," striving with the help of grace to do what is just and right. We are filled with awe at the wondrous plan of God, both at the way in which it is unfolding and at the future glory it promises.

Psalm 100

This psalm expresses the abundant joy the Christian feels on being redeemed by Christ. We have heard in the canticle of God's victory: every person will come to revere him. We know that Jesus too has risen from the dead and has opened for us the gates of paradise. In the psalm we call on "all the earth" to express its happiness to God. We are to serve him and to come happily into his presence. We have nothing to fear. "The Lord . . . is God" and we stand in a secure relationship to him. "He made us, we belong to him." There can be no sense of isolation or loneliness since all of us "belong" to God. Yes, we are "his people." His relation to us is that of a shepherd to his "flock." How greatly we can count on his protection.

Our response should be an eager one of going "within his gates" and entering "his courts." Our manner of doing so will be marked by gratitude and "songs of praise." What do we learn of God? He is "good." He loves us eternally. He is ever faithful.

From a Carmelite perspective we turn our gaze inward to God dwelling in our souls. We are to approach him "with joy"; we are to serve him "with gladness." This God who dwells in our souls "made us." We are encouraged to "go within his gates," to "enter his courts," singing and thanking him. Those "gates" and "courts" are in our hearts: there we will find him! Whom do we meet there? God who is good, showing "merciful love" and fidelity forever.

Reading: Ephesians 4:29-32

As we begin our day Paul gives us valuable advice on how we are to behave. Inwardly we are to avoid certain negative emotions and to replace them with positive ones. In making this change, we will discover that our speech and actions will be different.

How is it that we can act in an admirable way? In our hearts we have the Holy Spirit whom we received as a seal "against the day of redemption." It is this Spirit who will help us to imitate Jesus in our love for other people. We are to "get rid of all bitterness, all passion and anger." We are not to "let evil talk pass" our lips, no "harsh words," "slander" or "malice" of any kind. Our speech is to be uplifting. We are to say what people "need to hear," what will "really help them." In our actions we are to be "kind to one another, compassionate, and mutually forgiving." The wellspring for all such admirable behavior is our reception of forgiveness from Christ. If we act as St. Paul suggests, we will reflect Jesus in our lives and draw others to God.

Saturday

Psalm 119:145-152

With direct address I call on God "with all my heart." I ask him to "hear" me, to "save" me, and I promise to do his "will." I speak of how I spend my time, watching for God "through the night" and rising "before dawn" to call on him. I believe in God's love. I ask him to hear "my voice." The "decrees" of God are the source of "life" for me. I face enemies, but God is close. His commands are "truth." Since his will is firmly fixed, I am not afraid. It is this will that I long to do.

This lovely prayer brings us very close to God. He is there for us to call upon; he loves us; he gives us life; his will is "established for ever." The psalm becomes even richer from a Carmelite perspective. To God who dwells in my soul I cry out, asking him to hear me. I affirm that I will keep his "commands" and do his "will." Early in the morning and during the night I think of this God in my heart, crying for "help," hoping in his "word," and pondering his "promise." I believe that this God loves me and will "hear my voice." When he speaks his "decrees" within my heart, he gives me life. He inspires me to act in ways that please him, that match his will. I know that within myself there are forces that could harm me, and if I heed these and yield to them, I will act in ways far different from God's "law." I need not fear, however, because God is "close," in my very being. His "will is established" forever: what God plans for me and for everyone will occur. I rejoice because this God lives in my soul and wants to take me to paradise.

Canticle: Exodus 15:1-4a, 8-13, 17-18

The book of Exodus tells us that this canticle was the song of Moses and the Israelites after they crossed the Red Sea. We Christians sing the song joyously as we recall the glorious rescue from death of Jesus in the resurrection. We recall also that we have been saved from sin by our baptism. No inner foes, no sinfulness, can overwhelm us: God has given us victory in Jesus.

This song, written in the first person, resounds with joy. "I will sing to the Lord." In him are my "strength," "courage," and salvation. He deserves all my praise. In the case of the Israelites, he worked a great miracle. Enemies fell as waters stood high. The Israelites crossed on dry ground; the waters overwhelmed their pursuers. In our case, waters of baptism have swept away all the forces that can destroy our souls. God who worked these "wonders" is truly "magnificent in holiness."

God's help does not stop with this rescue. He led the Israelites to the "promised land." He guided their steps to the "sanctuary" which he had "established." This Lord "shall reign for ever and ever." So too, for us, the "new Israel," God has guided us to himself, the sanctuary of the Church. Over us he will always rule.

From a Carmelite perspective, we can go a level deeper with this wonderful song. We can see God, dwelling in the center of our souls, gloriously triumphing. There God is my "strength" and "courage." There he is my "savior" and "my God." All the evil impulses in myself, all my tendencies to sin, he overwhelms. He did so in baptism; he continues to do so in his care of me. Continually, he leads me, drawing my will to dwell at the center of my soul where he is. Each of us is a temple of God; each is the "sanctuary" he has "established." If we surrender in faith and love, God will "reign" over us "forever." And so we cry: "Who is like to you among the gods, O Lord? Who is like to you, magnificent in holiness?"

Psalm 117

In this exquisite psalm we call on "all . . . nations" to praise God. He deserves the acclaim of "all . . . peoples." Why? He loves us ! He is ever faithful! The psalm gives the grounds for our faith and hope. It leads us to love both God and neighbor. Because we have found God to be loving and faithful, we want all to share in our knowledge and joy. Wishing such good for our neighbors is true love for them.

Reading: 2 Peter 1:10-11

The reading calls on us to use our zeal to live a life of faith. If we do, we can hope, with confident expectation, to enter the "everlasting kingdom" of Jesus. The world so easily distracts our attention and draws us from the things of God. But we are looking forward to a "kingdom" that will last forever. Such a destiny should strengthen our will to live as Christians.

II: Evening Prayer

Sunday, Evening Prayer I

As we look at the four-week Psalter, we discern a traditional view of a day: it begins with sundown of one day and ends with sundown of the next. The Jewish people viewed the Sabbath in this way. The Church structures its prayer in the same fashion. This pattern becomes apparent with every Sunday and with all major feasts. On the first evening we say *Evening Prayer I;* on the second, *Evening Prayer II.*

As we approach these two *Hours,* we are curious to see what psalms and canticles the Church believes to be appropriate to begin and to end the Sunday of *Week I.* Somehow we expect to find themes related to our essence as human beings, our new identity in Christ, and the role of Jesus as savior. All these we find.

Psalm 141:1-9

At the beginning of this psalm, we find the lovely antiphon that could sum up the recitation of all the *Hours:*

> "Like burning incense, Lord, let my prayer rise up to you."

Like a fragrant offering, our prayer is to come to God. This psalm uses direct address, and in it we can hear our own voice and the voice of the Church.

As human beings, we have great need for God. In the past we have called upon him, and now we call again. We trust in his strength and wish God to use it quickly. Our hope is that for God our prayer is like "incense" and the raising of our hands, like an "evening oblation." Surely, if God is pleased with our prayer, his help will come.

We ask God to guard our speaking, for, as we well know, in words we can sin. We then go a level deeper: our hearts can turn to "things that are wrong." On one level the psalm in the next eight lines speaks of enemies outside ourselves with dire descriptions of the consequences of their actions. But we recognize in ourselves the attraction for "feasting" and "oil," that is, for deeds marked by evil and malice. We pray for the discernment to recognize as kindness words of reproof that may correct our behavior.

Our attention turns again to God. It is on him that we are to keep our eyes. God is our refuge and in him we find salvation. We pray to be kept from the evil that assails us both from without and from within.

From a Carmelite perspective we can turn our eyes inward. We direct our cries to God who abides in our hearts. We ask for his strength not to speak or act in a sinful way. We recognize the consequences of evil actions. It is to God within that our gaze is directed. There our refuge is to be found.

This psalm describes the essential state of human beings. We need God and his help. To him our prayer and oblation are due. We are capable of committing evil in speech and action, and the consequences of wickedness are to be clearly discerned. We human beings have God to gaze upon and to make a refuge. God is our hope. Thus we begin Week I with an awareness of who we are and who our helper is.

Psalm 142

In this psalm we pick up a theme we encountered also in the first psalm of this *Evening Prayer I*. God is our refuge. In Psalm 142 we can hear three voices, our own, that of the Church, and especially that of Jesus. We encounter in particular someone in great distress. At first we define our relationship to God. He is the one to whom I cry and make entreaty. I share my trouble and distress with him as my spirit faints. Then, in a moment of awakening, I say to God: "you . . . know my path."

As we look around, our situation seems desperate. Enemies are waiting; no ally is near; no escape is visible; no one cares. Now we address God directly, calling on him as our refuge and last resort in the "depths of distress." We ask for rescue and promise praise for deliverance. If we are saved, others will recognize the merciful action of God and "assemble" around us. Our condition then will differ greatly from the terrible loneliness in which we now find ourselves.

This psalm, like the previous one, clarifies our human position. In trouble and anguish God is our refuge. He is the one who can rescue us, especially when we feel abandoned or under siege. We can sense too that joy will be ours when we find that God has rescued us from our distress.

From a Carmelite perspective we can turn to God within our souls. What a joy to know that he is there in times of desperate trouble! Who are our enemies? They may be external. Perhaps, however, they are negative traits of self, negative passions or feelings, that harass us from within. In the face of these we feel especially vulnerable. In our interior suffering we cry out to God for rescue. When he brings our soul out of the prison of "self," then we are filled with praise and others recognize the action of divine grace in our souls.

How is this psalm the voice of Jesus? Hilary (c. 315—c. 368) saw in it aspects of Christ's passion, as the sentence preceding the psalm states. Truly we can hear Jesus crying out in anguish as his enemies attack him. He trusts the Father completely as he sees no one to help him. He is in utter distress. He calls for rescue; he wants his soul saved from "prison." And the Father hears! In the resurrection Jesus is called forth in anguish from the tomb! In hearing the voice of Jesus in this psalm and in recalling his victory over death, we see why this psalm is found in *Evening Prayer I* for

Sunday. On this day Jesus rises! We recall, however, the dread suffering that preceded the resurrection. Our love for our Savior deepens. Jesus has allowed us to be in the number of the "just" who "assemble" around him because of the Father's "goodness" to him. He justified us by his sufferings; we rejoice at his resurrection.

Canticle: Philippians 2:6-11

The canticle takes up the theme of the previous psalm when it is heard as the voice of Jesus. We hear of how Jesus became our Savior. He, being "in the form of God," did not hold on to his divinity. Paul tells us that Jesus was willing to "*empty* himself" of this divinity for our sake. He chose the human state and in that state descended even further to the point of accepting death as a criminal. Paul focuses on the tremendous emptying of Jesus to which we too are called. We are to lose our *selves* for his sake as he did for ours. The Father now has exalted Jesus, and every human being must adore him. One truth exceeds all others: Jesus is Lord!

This canticle gives us the focus for our whole life: Jesus. We hear of the cost of the incarnation. We recall the terrible death of Jesus. We learn that Jesus has acquired once again his divinity. When we acknowledge Jesus as Lord, the Father is glorified.

Reading: Romans 11:33-36

Paul offers two exclamations about the nature of God. He speaks of different characteristics—riches, wisdom, knowledge—and notes their depth. God's judgments are inscrutable; his ways are unsearchable. Quoting, then, apparently from Isaiah 40:13 and Job 41:3 (although these references are not completely certain), Paul describes the human situation. Who among us can claim to know God's mind? Which human being has ever offered him advice? Who has ever given God a gift for which he would deserve a gift from God in return? Paul then states the exact truth of the universe: all things have their origin in God, are sustained by God, and exist for his purposes alone. Thus all glory is properly his forever.

With the three questions that Paul asks we can perceive the temptations that human beings can face. Do we imagine that we know God's mind? Do we, in our lives, sometimes feel that we could counsel God about what would be best in our circumstances? Do we suppose that all our service or gifts to him make some positive return mandatory? We can make such assumptions, forgetting who we are as creatures and to whom all things belong.

Yet the truth dawns brightly! As we surrender our will and desires to God, we encounter mystery. God's riches, wisdom, and knowledge are "deep." His judgments are "inscrutable," his ways "unsearchable." As human beings we can never understand God's thoughts or ways.

With this reading on the wonder and unfathomable nature of God, we begin Week I of the *Hours.* How well chosen the psalms, canticle, and reading are to clarify who we are and who God is! In awe at God's power, wisdom, and glory, we gratefully realize our position as human beings redeemed by the generous sacrifice of Jesus. We have heard the cries of his suffering. Gratefully we bend the knee and say, "Jesus is Lord!"

Sunday, Evening Prayer II

Psalm 110:1-5, 7

This psalm is a Messianic psalm, speaking of the power and nature of the Messiah. We can hear, from a Christian point of view, the Father speaking to Jesus. He assigns to Jesus a position of honor: "on my right." He promises that all who oppose Jesus, "the way and the truth and the life" (John 14:6), will come eventually to recognize his sovereignty. We may suppose that they will do so in love and gratitude. We learn who Jesus is: "a prince" from the day of his birth. As we read these words, how we recall the message of Gabriel to Mary about Jesus: "He will be great and will be called Son of the Most High, and the Lord God will give him the throne of David his father, and he will rule over the house of Jacob forever, and of his kingdom there will be no end" (Luke 1:32-33).

The next line, "from the womb before the dawn I begot you," again recalls the incarnation of Jesus. We remember the words to Mary: "The holy Spirit will come upon you, and the power of the Most High will over-shadow you" (Luke 1:35). The Father has endowed Jesus with an identity that is "for ever": he is a priest like "Melchizedek of old." Jesus is always a priest, interceding for his people. The Father will ever take care of Jesus. His enemies will fall; he will be victorious. The last two lines are obscure, but the image is that of Jesus being refreshed.

In this psalm of *Sunday, Week I,* we again find the *Hours* focusing our attention on essentials. Jesus is the center of our lives, chosen to be such by the Father. We can rejoice endlessly in who Jesus is. He has the "scepter." He is "prince." He is under the Father's protection. He will ever be our "priest," interceding for and redeeming his people.

In this psalm we do not hear the usual voices speaking, ours, the Church's, or that of Jesus. Instead, we have a description of how the Father regards Jesus. He gives Jesus the position on his "right"; he makes Jesus a "priest for ever."

From a Carmelite perspective, we recall that Jesus abides in our hearts. This psalm helps us to appreciate who it is who rules within and why he does so. Jesus is "prince"; Jesus is "priest." He ever redeems us and governs us with love. The Father wants us always to hear his beloved Son, as he made clear at the Transfiguration (Matthew 17:5): "This is my beloved Son . . . ; listen to him." We know that the Father will help and refresh Jesus as he lives within our souls.

Psalm 114

This psalm is one of sheer joy! As we end our Sunday, we look back over the day with gratitude. What help from God can we discern that we have received during this day? Are we drawn to glance back at our life as a whole and recognize the loving providence of God within it? Israel had wandered in the desert for many, long years. During this time God had fed and protected his people, but, oh! how they longed for the promised land. And then the moment for entry came. It was a time of new identity: "Judah became the Lord's temple, Israel became his kingdom." All nature was filled with delight. The Jordan parted its waters, and the people crossed on dry land into their new home.

What a splendid image the psalmist offers! "The mountains leapt like rams and the hills like yearling sheep." To reinforce the images, he asks the sea, mountains, and hills why they behaved in this way. The answer is found in the last stanza. God is with his people and, at his presence, wondrous events occur. In the past God gave his people water in the desert (Exodus 17:6; Numbers 20:11) by working miracles. So now the earth should "tremble" because the "God of Jacob" is here.

As in the previous psalm, we do not hear in this psalm the three voices, ours, the Church's, or that of Jesus. We find instead the description of an exquisite moment of joy. God has brought his people home. And we, as the new Israel, belong to that people!

From the Carmelite perspective, this psalm may describe the boundless joy that the soul feels when it discovers during this life its true home: God dwelling at its very center. In light of this truth, the soul realizes that it is "the Lord's temple"; it is "his kingdom." Everything within reacts with joy. Our whole being delights in this truth. It should "tremble" also because the God who works miracles is present.

Canticle: Based on Revelation 19:1-7

This canticle is filled with the sound of Easter: "Alleluia." We Christians are people of the resurrection. We cannot help crying out "Alleluia," that is, "Praise God!" The canticle ascribes to God his due: salvation, glory, and power. We recognize the nature of his actions: "honest and true." Our role as human beings is constantly to offer praise with rejoicing. The final stanza describes what is happening in heaven: "the wedding feast" of Jesus has begun. We are the "bride." What we are doing is making ourselves ready for his return.

As our Sunday comes to a close, we are given our mission as we face a new week of work and encounters. We are to make ourselves ready to welcome Jesus. The reference in Revelation is clearly to the second coming of Jesus. We can extend it, however, to include the way in which we meet our neighbor: in each we can "welcome" Jesus.

Reading: 2 Corinthians 1:3-4

The themes from the canticle recur in the reading. We owe praise to the Father. Now we focus on two of his gifts: "mercies" and "consolation." Our receipt of these gifts, we discover, makes us ready for a mission. We are to use the consolation we receive to console others. The gifts we have received transform us into their own essence, and we can become "consolation" for others. This is our cause for joy as we begin a new week. God gives us mercy and consolation; we can then give them to our neighbor. Armed with such generous gifts from God, we can joyfully welcome Jesus in all whom we meet.

Monday

Psalm 11

We have finished our first day of work for this week. In this psalm we can hear three voices: our own, that of the Church, and that of Jesus. We begin by stating our position: it is in the Lord that we take "refuge." We need not, like frightened birds, fly off to a mountain. True, the world we encounter is filled with evil. We may feel helpless before it. If our foundations are destroyed, what can we do?

Yet we need have no fear. God is in charge of the universe. He knows the actions of all people. The wicked will receive punishment but the "upright" one day will gaze on his face.

This is a psalm that becomes very effective if we use direct address to God.

In *you, Lord,* I have taken my refuge.

. . .

You, Lord, are in your holy temple,
you, whose throne is in heaven.
Your eyes look down on the world;
your gaze tests mortal men.

You test the just and the wicked:
the lover of violence *you hate.*
You send fire and brimstone on the wicked;
you send a scorching wind as their lot.

You, Lord, are just and *love* justice:
the upright shall see *your* face.

We meet God as our refuge, as our guardian, as the judge of our actions. As we finish our day's work, we hope that we have loved "justice." Our longing is to "see his face."

Reading this psalm from a Carmelite perspective, we find a splendid picture of the God who dwells within. The psalm becomes a personal encounter with God. God is our refuge; he reigns within. He looks at our inner nature. We know that we can be "just" or "wicked." Such a range is in all of us. But the psalm emphasizes that it is justice that God wishes. He himself is "just and loves justice." We will strive, therefore, to imitate him within. If we are "upright," we may also come to gaze on him within.

Psalm 15

As we look back over our day, we may ask: Did we act in a worthy way? The previous psalm has given us the hope of a divine encounter, but for whom will this be possible? In direct address we ask God who will come into his presence. We then find a description of the person who will have this privilege. Let us summarize this person's features. First, we hear of personal characteristics: walking without fault, acting with justice, speaking the truth from the heart, not slandering with the tongue. We find, therefore, virtue, justice, and two kinds of speech, true and never vicious.

Second, we learn how we are to treat our neighbor: we do not wrong or slander anyone and honor those who love God. In the community we prove faithful. In regard to money we are honest.

From a Carmelite perspective, we learn what will help us to find God within our souls. We see what we should strive for in our attitudes and behavior. Inwardly, we aim for virtue: justice, truth, pure speech. Outwardly, we love our neighbor and act with integrity. These actions on our part can prepare us for the inner journey. They do not guarantee it, but they can help to make it possible.

Canticle: Ephesians 1:3-10

The psalms have taught us who God is and who will be privileged to approach him. The canticle now tells us why we human beings can hope for such blessings. In this lovely opening of Ephesians, Paul speaks eloquently of our great calling in Christ. In him the Father has given us "every spiritual blessing." Think on this! There is no spiritual blessing that we lack. From the Carmelite point of view the greatest blessing is our awareness that God dwells at the center of our soul. This state is possible because of Christ's redemptive actions.

Then we learn that God chose us before the universe was created and called us to be "holy" and "blameless in his sight." Thus, long before any of us appeared on earth, God had a plan for us. Our destiny is to be "holy." When the Father looks at us, he sees us as "blameless." This view of us is possible because of our redemption in Christ. We were predestined to be "adopted" children. Our response to this privilege is to praise endlessly the "glorious favor" God has bestowed on us. Always we are aware that this free gift of grace has come through Jesus Christ who shed his blood for us.

God has granted us yet another great gift: to understand the mystery of our redemption. Before the universe began God planned to save us in Jesus who became a human being "in the fulness of time." The result will be that "all things" will be brought "into one" in Jesus. Truly this wondrous Savior is the center of creation and of our lives.

In this canticle we hear our voice and that of the Church. Its message to us is profound. We may find this message even more enhanced if we use direct address to the Father in some lines. "Praised be *you*, God and Father" (3). "*You*, God, chose us in him" (4). "*You* predestined us . . . that all might praise the glorious favor *you have* bestowed on us in *the* beloved" (5-6). "*You have* given us the wisdom to understand fully the mystery" (9). This canticle tells us of a personal relationship with God. Each of us was loved and chosen long before the universe appeared. Each of us has been redeemed, receiving God's glorious grace. In awe and thanksgiving we bless the Father for his gift of Christ. We enter into his presence, recalling his rich gifts to us and blessing him with all our hearts.

Reading: Colossians 1:9b-11

The reading echoes what we have heard in the canticle. There we learned that God gave us the "wisdom" to understand what he "was pleased to decree in Christ." Now Paul prays that we may know God's will "through perfect wisdom and spiritual insight." We have heard of the grand design God had to redeem the world. Now we need "wisdom" and "insight" to find our part of God's will, his will for our own lives. If we accept and obey God's will, our lives will be "worthy of the Lord and pleasing to him in every way." The effects will be two: we will perform "good works" and "grow in the knowledge of God."

If we gain "full knowledge of God's will through perfect wisdom and spiritual insight," God will fill us with the "might of his glory." We will find within "the strength needed to stand fast." We may find more: joy to endure "whatever may come." This strength and joy are manifestations of the presence of God, marks of his glory. The presence of these astounds us and makes our hardships less harrowing. God is with us. We can stand firm.

If we read this passage from a Carmelite perspective, we can focus on the wondrous nature of the soul. Through prayer, focusing on God within our souls, we may acquire "perfect wisdom and spiritual insight." The consequence will be that we learn "God's will" and perform "good works." We will grow ever in the "knowledge of God," finding "strength" to face all trials and hardships. All these gifts—wisdom, insight, knowledge, strength—will fill our souls and pour forth in love for others.

Tuesday

Psalm 20

This lovely psalm is an extended prayer for us. We can hear in the requests the voice of the Church or the voice of Jesus for his people. We have lived and worked through our day and perhaps we have met with suffering and distress. The first prayer for us is that God will hear our cry in trouble and protect us. We are to receive help and support as God remembers our past gifts.

The next prayer is that our "heart's desire" and "plans" be fulfilled. If all goes well, we will be victorious, just as the Lord's anointed will be. From the Christian perspective we know that Jesus has won the victory over sin and death by his passion and resurrection.

The psalmist tells us that some people falsely place trust in sources of strength other than the Lord. We, however, trust in God and "we shall hold and stand firm." As Christians, we again rejoice because Jesus has been victorious. We pray that when we are in need, God will help us.

This psalm, as our day ends, speaks lovingly to our hearts. We hear prayers that all our endeavors of the day will prove successful. We hear also pleas for help in case our day has brought trials. We encounter a hope that we will be victorious in what we have undertaken. We can be confident for the future because we place our trust in God. In him is our strength and stability.

Psalm 21:2-8,14

If we read this psalm from a Christian perspective, it can give us great joy as we rejoice at the victory of

Jesus. We know that Jesus has been victorious over death. How he suffered for our sakes! But death could not defeat him. As we say this psalm, we may envision Jesus at the moment of his resurrection. What joy must have filled his heart!

"You have granted him his heart's desire." On the cross Jesus entrusted his spirit to his Father. His trust was not misplaced, for the Father raised him to life again. The Father came to meet Jesus with "blessings of success." "He asked you for life and this you have given, days that will last from age to age." Jesus is risen and will live forever! The Father greatly blessed him, and us, by raising him from the dead. Truly Jesus has received "glory," "majesty and splendor." He has received the Father's "blessings" forever.

Now Jesus is with the Father: he rejoices with the "joy" of his presence. Jesus trusted the Father and will ever "stand firm." We honor the Father for his "strength" and "power." His goodness to us makes us break into song.

How appropriate is this psalm for *Evening Prayer!* Our whole focus is on Jesus, and in this psalm we can share his joy, his triumph, his victory over death. Our happiness lies in seeing how the Father loved and loves him. This Jesus is our king and savior. In hearing of his blessings and sharing in his delight, we are invited to turn our attention from ourselves, to adopt a cosmic view and to rejoice that Jesus is the victorious king over the universe which he has redeemed.

Canticle: Revelation 4:11; 5:9,10,12

This canticle gives verses from Revelation that describe the heavenly court. First, we have the praise offered to the Father by the twenty-four elders. He deserves "glory and honor and power" because he has created and still sustains all living beings. Second, we hear of Jesus, the Lamb of God, who deserves the highest honor because he died to redeem us. He has conferred on us the highest dignity, making us "a kingdom and priests." We are to "reign on earth." To Jesus belongs, therefore, "power," "riches," "wisdom," "strength," "honor," "glory," and "praise." There is no wonderful thing that he does not deserve.

This canticle focuses our eyes on Jesus. We exult in his triumph. We are overwhelmed with gratitude. We are summoned to give him all, our hearts filled with love.

Reading: 1 John 3:1a, 2

John speaks of the wondrous love God has shown us in allowing us to "be called" his "children." This title suggests a close, intimate relationship marked by affection and fidelity. But John promises us more. Already we are "children." When we see God, we shall become "like him." The mystery and wonder of this strike us with amazement. Somehow we are to be transformed into the very image of God. We do not know what this change will involve. We can only be overwhelmed with gratitude at what God plans for us.

Wednesday

Psalm 27–I

This psalm is written in the first person, and we can hear our own voice and the voice of the Church. We can hear also the voice of Jesus as he speaks within our hearts to his Father. Who is the Lord? "My light and my help." How personal the references to "my" are! They emphasize that each of us has an individual relationship with God. No human being can cause us fear since God is our "light," "help," and "stronghold." Our relationship with God, however, does not prevent attacks but, when these occur, it is our enemies who are defeated. Even in extreme circumstances our hearts can be free from fear and we can trust.

The psalmist then expresses his deepest longing, the one request he makes of the Lord: to live his whole life in the Lord's "house," savoring his "sweetness" and beholding his "temple." Is this not the strongest desire in each of us also? The psalmist then gives us the reason for his longing. God keeps him safe when evil threatens. He can stand free from his enemies and offer "a sacrifice of joy." His whole response will be one of singing and dancing. When we feel God's protection holding us close and keeping us safe, our hearts burst with joy. He makes us wish to sing.

From a Carmelite point of view, this psalm tells of the wondrous presence of God within the soul. The Lord lives in our heart as our "light and help." He is our "stronghold." What we may fear often is our own self, the evil tendencies that emerge and never quite disappear. But, before the presence of God, these vanish. If we are with God in our souls, nothing can make our hearts afraid or disturb our trust.

One longing we have: to stay with this Divine Guest at each moment. We wish to "savor his sweetness" and to "behold his temple." Yes, this temple is in our very soul! Ah, there, we can hide and be safe. There we triumph over our sins and we are filled with joy. We offer this joy as our sacrifice. Inwardly we sing and adore.

Psalm 27–II

This psalm continues with a direct prayer to God: "hear" me; "answer." Our hearts tell us: "seek his face." We tell God that we look for him. We do not wish somehow to miss him, to find his "face" hidden. It is God who is our "help." Then we realize a profound truth: every human being may abandon us, even our parents, but God is always there, always ready to welcome and "receive" us.

We now speak directly to God, telling him we want to walk in his way. We hope that this way is "even." Life holds many dangers, but our call is to hope in God's mercy and love now. Buoyed up by hope, we can "hold firm and take heart."

From a Carmelite perspective, these verses again fill us with wonder at God's presence within. We address this God in our hearts: "hear my voice when I call; have mercy and answer." We believe firmly that God is there; we wait for his inner urgings and directives. Our hearts, the center and core of our being, have urged us in this way: "seek his face." Yes, he is within! Yes, he can be found! We do not want to find him hidden. We know that he has helped us in the past. All others may leave us, but at our hearts' core God will ever receive us. Because he is there, we ask God to instruct us and to be our guide. We may encounter within ourselves evil tendencies that shatter our serenity and peace. We are confident that we shall encounter God's goodness within our very being. We are to put our full hope in God who is in our hearts.

Canticle: Colossians 1:12-20

In this canticle we fix our eyes on Jesus to see who he is. Our basic attitude is one of gratitude. We have been found "worthy to share the lot of the saints in light." We know that this is true because of what Jesus has done for us. Before we were under "the power of darkness." We now live elsewhere: "in the kingdom of his beloved Son." Our state has changed: our sins have been forgiven.

Jesus is the "image of the invisible God." In regard to creation he holds first place of power and supremacy. Being the wisdom of God and his Word, Christ is at the center of all creation: "in him everything in heaven and on earth was created." Jesus is the source of creation and the end for which created things were made: "through him . . . for him." "He is before all else that is": so we hear in the Gospel of John that Jesus existed before creation (1:1; 8:58). Creation was made through Jesus and is sustained by him.

Jesus is "head of the body, the church." We have not only been saved but made part of a new "body" with a "head" who is God. In every way Jesus is first. In particular this is so of his being the first human being to be resurrected from the dead. In Jesus is "absolute fulness." The Father has reconciled "everything" in Jesus by one means: the death of Jesus on the cross. His blood has bought us "peace."

If we use direct address for portions of this canticle, we can draw very close to Jesus:

You are the image of the invisible God. . . .
In *you* everything . . . was created. . . .

All were created through *you;*
all were created for *you.*
You are before all else that is.
In *you* everything continues in being.

It is *you who are* head of the body, the church!
you who are the beginning . . .
so that primacy may be *yours* in everything.

It pleased God to make absolute fullness reside in
    you
and, by means of *you,* to reconcile everything in
    your person . . .
making peace through the blood of *your* cross.

Using direct address in this way, we encounter Jesus in an intimate fashion. We learn vividly of his nature, his relationship to creation, to us as Church, and to the Father. We hear of what his death has accomplished. How we are summoned to reverence and awe of our wondrous Redeemer!

Reading: James 1:22, 25

Listening to the canticle, we have been given a view of how Jesus has changed our lives. James gives us a warning: it is not sufficient simply to hear about Jesus. We must act on the truth the gospel presents. We are called to look on "freedom's ideal law," that is, the full gospel message, and reflect it to the world. In this way we leave the realm of darkness and bring light to the world.

Thursday

Psalm 30

In this psalm we speak in our own voice with joy for God's rescue of us. God has saved me! My enemies have not been able to "rejoice over me." I was in danger! I needed healing. It was the Lord who "healed me" and brought me to life again.

I have learned about God from my experience. His "anger" is momentary, his "favor" persistent. Yes, we may encounter situations that bring "tears," but joy soon follows. I have learned more about myself from my experience. In "good fortune" I imagined that nothing could harm me. It was God's favor that had put me "on a mountain fastness," but I failed to recognize the source of my blessings. When God "hid" his face, my confidence and self-assurance were shattered. "I was put to confusion."

And then I cried out to God! I begged him to save me from death. And he did! God showed mercy. Now, instead of "mourning," I engage in "dancing." I am "clothed . . . with joy," determined to please God forever.

On an inner level this psalm can help us through times of dryness and aridity in prayer. On our spiritual journey we can experience periods of darkness. Enemies from within seem to gain the upper hand—discouragement, despair, loneliness, a sense of abandonment. Then we cry out to God and he rescues us, bringing joy and meaning again to our lives.

Perhaps too at times we become too confident, not realizing that we are trusting in our own strength, forgetting the working of grace. God then seems to become absent and spiritually we come close to death. God takes pity on our weakness and makes his presence felt once again. How we rejoice!

In this psalm too we can travel with Jesus through the passion to his resurrection. Yes, the Father rescued him from death! His enemies did not triumph! The Father heard the impassioned cry of Jesus for help on the cross and raised him from the dead on the third day: "joy" came "with the dawn." Jesus, now risen, is "clothed . . . with joy." His soul expresses endless praise and thanks to the Father.

Psalm 32

As we end our day, we glance back over our activities. Like all human beings, we are sinners and perhaps the day has found us not acting at our best. This psalm tells us how to act in this situation. Joy can be ours because we have a God who forgives. When our "offense is forgiven," our "sin is remitted," we are happy! When we no longer feel "guilt," and when no "guile" stains our souls, yes, we are happy!

Speaking in the first person, the psalmist describes what happens when we retain our sins and keep them secret. What do I experience? Poor health, inner groanings, loss of strength. I sense God's displeasure: "your hand *is* heavy upon me.

How different my condition after confessing my sins! "I . . . acknowledged my sins." I revealed my guilt. And, wonder of wonders, God forgave not merely the sins but the guilt they caused.

Our experience makes us call others to prayer to God. No matter how threatening circumstances may seem, we shall be safe. We can hide in God and we find ourselves wrapped around, as it were, with the "cries of deliverance" we utter.

Then in the psalm we hear God speaking directly to us. As we have turned from our sins and confessed them to God, we have felt a profound joy. But God then promises to do more for us: "I will instruct you and teach you the way you should go; I will give you counsel with my eye upon you." God wants to help us on our way, to guide us so that we will not sin or fall into danger. He urges us not to be stubborn. He wants to save us from the "sorrows" that the wicked have. He tells us that those who trust him will experience his "loving mercy."

What can our response be to such a God as this? Our cry is "rejoice, rejoice!" He makes us "just" and "upright of heart," knowing that, being such, we will be filled with joy.

From a Carmelite perspective, we can see all that this psalm describes as taking place within our own being. We sin and then we languish. We confess our guilt and God fills us with happiness. We should, therefore, in time of temptation and danger, cry out to God who abides at the center of our souls. We can make God there our "hiding place." We find our souls surrounded, as it were, by our own "cries of deliverance."

God speaks to us within our hearts, telling us that he will "instruct," "teach," and "counsel" us. But we must listen; we must not resist. We must come near to God. And what will we find if we trust in his presence within? "Loving mercy." Dwelling in God as our "hiding place," we will be "just" and "upright of heart." What gladness will be ours!

Canticle: Revelation 11:17-18; 12:10b-12a

In these lines we hear the song of praise of those redeemed by Christ. With his passion, death, and resurrection a new era began and continues to unfold. For ages human beings had rebelled, but God intervened in history. Now all who proved faithful, "the great and the small alike," can hope for a reward. All is changed for human beings because "salvation and power" have come. God reigns! Jesus, the "Anointed One," has "authority." Finally the "accuser," who brought our sins ever to God's attention, has been stripped of his power. What defeated him was the "blood of the Lamb." Those now in heaven testified to Christ and did not cling to life. Joy fills heaven because they have triumphed.

These lines teach us so much about the Christian faith! We praise God "who is and who was." We believe that this God reigns. He has control over the nations no matter what their behavior. He is the one who judges the dead and gives a reward. Jesus is the "Anointed One" who has "authority." Satan, ever blaming human beings, is "cast out." Christians are washed in the "blood of the Lamb." Their strength comes from "the word of their testimony" and their hope of life after death. Christianity promises rejoicing in heaven for those who believe.

Reading: 1 Peter 1:6-9

The canticle has described the joy to be found in heaven. Peter tells us of the "cause for rejoicing" that we have here on earth. We are on a spiritual journey. Yes, "trials" will come that bring "distress." But these trials have a purpose. Peter urges us to see them in a particular light, to call them even "a cause of rejoicing." What do trials do? They test our faith. This faith is our most valuable possession: "more precious than the passing splendor of fire-tried gold." If trials prove our faith genuine, we have a great hope: "praise, glory, and honor when Jesus Christ appears."

Who is Jesus Christ? Him whom we love, even though we have "never seen him." "Without seeing," we believe in Jesus. What is our state because we do this? We "rejoice with inexpressible joy touched with glory." The cause for our joy is that faith has the goal of "salvation" and we are achieving this. Our joy is thus "touched with glory."

The reading presents essential elements of our Christian journey. We believe in Jesus Christ whom we have "never seen." We "love" him. We have "faith," our most valuable possession which gives us hope of "salvation." "Trials" in life bring great "distress," but we see these trials in a new way, one that makes us "rejoice with inexpressible joy touched with glory." We know that our faith is being made genuine and that its "goal" is becoming more and more sure. Already our joy becomes one beyond words, partaking in "glory" because of what is happening to and within our souls. Jesus whom we love will appear and then we will find "praise, glory, and honor." Our faith has given us meaning in life and a totally new way of facing whatever trials may come.

Friday

Psalm 41

This psalm, partly in direct address, expresses a reflection on our relationship with God, especially in time of distress. The psalmist suggests that the best way we can act is to take thought for "the poor and the weak." If we do, then the Lord will protect us in various circumstances in our lives, especially when we are sick.

We will be "happy," dwelling ever under the Lord's saving help. The second thing we must do is to recognize our own sinfulness: we pray to God for mercy since it is against him that we have "sinned."

The psalmist then describes the agony we experience when enemies attack us and friends turn against us. We pray to God for mercy, knowing that with his assistance we "shall be unharmed" and shall enjoy the privilege of being in his "presence for evermore."

For us Christians, one line strikes a discord: "Let me rise once more and I will repay them." Jesus has taught us to forgive, and in the Lord's Prayer we ask for forgiveness only in the degree that we have forgiven. Jesus himself on the cross said: "Father, forgive them, they know not what they do" (Luke 23:34). We are called, therefore, as Christians, to bear with forgiving hearts the sufferings inflicted by others. We recognize our own sinfulness and know that our help will come from our merciful and living God.

Parts of this psalm tell us much about Jesus. He was one who ever considered "the poor and the weak." In the description of enemies making an attack, we can see the experience of Jesus. How we can sympathize with the agony of his passion and especially for his suffering over the betrayal of Judas! We all, by our sins, crucified him, but the Father raised him from the dead. For our sakes Jesus became "sin" (2 Corinthians 5:21) in order to take all our sins away. Jesus fulfills what the psalm describes: "happy" is he in his victory on our behalf!

Psalm 46

This wonderful psalm tells us what strong confidence we can have because of who God is. It contains a refrain that emphasizes its theme: "The Lord of hosts is with us: the God of Jacob is our stronghold." We are never alone but in the constant presence of God. He acts as a "stronghold": we can, as it were, dwell within God and be totally safe.

Stanza one tells us who God is: "a refuge and strength, a helper close at hand, in times of distress." How those words encourage us to pray, to place ourselves in God's presence and to draw on his power! When danger threatens, he is there, right at our side. No kind of disaster can daunt us. The psalmist describes alarming natural calamities, but even these are not to be feared.

Stanza two describes the dwelling of God. His presence makes this dwelling unshakable: Jerusalem is a safe haven. If it is threatened, the mere sound of God's voice removes all danger. God is there to help "at the dawning of the day."

Stanza three urges us to see the "works of the Lord." He brings an end to all types of hostility, destroying the weapons human beings have made. God calls on us to be at peace within and to recognize who he is: "Be still and know that I am God, supreme among the nations, supreme on the earth!"

If we read this psalm from a Carmelite point of view, we draw very close to God abiding in the core of our being. In our hearts God is a "refuge and strength, a helper close at hand, in time of distress." How could he be closer than in our very souls? To him, in willing surrender, we can come as a "refuge." From him we can draw "strength." No matter what happens outside our bodies, God is "with us"; he is our "stronghold."

Our souls are now "God's city." They cannot be "shaken." Each day God helps us and, at his voice, all else fades away. How does God work within us? He removes all hostile elements. We can live for him. He urges us to "be still" and to let him be "supreme" in our whole nature.

Canticle: Revelation 15:3-4

In these lines we have "the song of Moses, the servant of God, and the song of the Lamb" (Revelation 15: 3a, not part of text chosen). Christians, like the ancient Hebrews, have crossed into the Promised Land, saved by the sacrifice of Jesus, the Lamb of God. We sing a song of triumph, acknowledging the God who from the beginning planned the salvation of the human race through all its stages. God is "Almighty." His works are "mighty and wonderful," especially those of salvation. His ways are "righteous and true." What he has done is upright; what he is by nature is truth. All people must recognize the "honor" and "glory" that are due to this wondrous God. Our role as human beings is to give worship to what is holy. Only God is "holy" and all nations "shall come and worship" in his presence. We will ponder and consider his mighty deeds, filled ever with greater and greater awe.

In these lines we may hear the voice of Jesus praising God the Father, especially after his resurrection from the dead. Look at what the Father has done in raising Jesus! With what joy Jesus may speak of the Father's "mighty and wonderful . . . works," and his "righteous and true . . . ways." "All nations" will come to give "honor" and "glory" and worship in the Father's presence. With Jesus, we have seen the "mighty deeds" of God, and with him we loudly acclaim the One who worked out our salvation.

Reading: Romans 15:1-3

In this passage Paul teaches us how to relate to those whose faith may be less strong than our own. Our focus has to be on what is best for the other person. We are to strive to benefit others, thus "building up" their spirit.

In acting in this way we will imitate Jesus. Paul quotes from Psalm 69:9: "The reproaches they uttered against you fell on me." Jesus took on himself the "reproaches uttered against" the Father. To remove these, Jesus was willing to die on the cross for us. In acting with others, then, we should forget any superiority that we might feel and quietly work for their good.

2.
Week II: Morning and Evening Prayer

*In the rays of dawn and sunset
your radiant loveliness shines forth.*

I: Morning Prayer

Sunday

Psalm 118

As we begin our prayer of Sunday morning, our hearts thrill with the knowledge of our own salvation and with joy at the resurrection of Jesus. On one level, we can pray this psalm with our own voice. We address God directly and this brings us close to him. What we realize first is that God loves us always. The love of God "endures for ever." We are so overwhelmed with this knowledge that we want to share it with the whole world. Let everyone say: God's "love endures for ever." Once in the past God saved me from my foes; so he will do in the future: I am not afraid of my foes.

I have learned to trust the Lord, not earthly powers. God is my best "refuge" and best source of strength. With this strength I became victorious, and now I want to sing. I recognize God's activity: "his right hand raised me." I shall live. Yes, what has happened to me I may consider as a "punishment" because I have sinned. This I know. But death did not come. I am alive and can praise God for his gift of life to me.

Now I have come to long for one thing: holiness. If I am allowed to enter, I will "thank you!" I address God directly, expressing my gratitude: "you are my savior!"

I have been like a "stone . . . rejected," but now I am like a "corner stone." This change had nothing to do with me:

it was all God's work. This day of gladness is God's gift. From him: salvation, success, light. My response to God is: "I thank you . . . I praise you!" Once again I say with joyful exhilaration: God's love "endures forever."

On a second level this psalm is a glorious resurrection anthem of Jesus. In Matthew 21:42 Jesus quotes the lines about the "stone . . . rejected," referring to himself. At Acts 4:11 likewise Peter calls Jesus the "stone" that has become "the cornerstone." Our *Hours* quote this passage at the head of the psalm. We can hear, therefore, the voice of Jesus expressing his joy at his resurrection.

First, Jesus calls upon all of us to recognize that God's "love endures for ever." Then he recalls his passion. At this time he was in distress. He took "refuge in the Lord." He overcame all who were attacking him. God was ever by his side. God triumphed in raising Jesus from the dead. It was for our sins and offenses that he "was punished" but God's "right hand raised" Jesus. After the resurrection and ascension Jesus entered heaven: for him the "gates of holiness" were opened. God has taken the "stone which the builders rejected" and made it the "corner stone." Truly, this is a marvel!

The next two lines of the psalm we often associate with Sunday, the day of resurrection:

This day was made by the Lord;
we rejoice and are glad.

Through the power of the resurrection, we have all received salvation. Truly we say of Jesus: "Blessed in the name of the Lord is he who comes." This was the song of those who greeted Jesus as he entered Jerusalem on Palm Sunday. In Matthew 23:39 Jesus says that these words are what believers will say of him. At each Eucharist we proclaim these words before the consecration: "Blessed is he who comes," still comes to save his people.

As the psalm closes, <u>Jesus calls on his people</u> to come forward "<u>with branches</u>." We are to acclaim the risen Jesus at his altar. With him now we thank God, proclaiming that "his love endures for ever."

From a Carmelite perspective, <u>we can journey inward in this psalm.</u> God dwells within, his love enduring forever. There, at the center of my soul, I cried to him when I was in distress. He "answered and freed me." How wise to take refuge in God within, better than trusting in people no matter how powerful.

Within myself I find negative traits and sources of sinfulness. Those often become my "attackers." But God saves me and gives me cause for joy. My sinfulness brings me suffering, but God gives me life.

<u>Within my soul itself are "gates of holiness." This holiness is the presence of God within</u>. Imbued with grace, I can enter into this inner temple which truly belongs to the Lord. <u>Jesus is the cornerstone of this temple</u>. How I rejoice at his "day," the day of his triumphant resurrection. How joyfully I say: "Blessed in the name of the Lord is he who comes." Jesus dwells within my soul and there I honor him. Surely we can say of this God who chooses to dwell within my soul: "his love endures for ever."

Canticle: Daniel 3:52-57

As in *Sunday, Week I,* the canticle again comes from Daniel. We encounter a wondrous list of different aspects of God. Once again this is given to us as part of <u>the song of the three young men in the fiery furnace.</u> We are astonished at their response when they are in extreme danger. But they know that they are not, for the flames do not hurt them and a cooling breeze delights. In their absolute joy at knowing that God protects them, they sing that he deserves praise because of who he is. For many reasons God is "praiseworthy and exalted above all forever." This line in their song becomes a response that appears after each line of description.

What are God's attributes? He is "blessed"; so is his name; so is his dwelling. He is "blessed" as he gazes on his creation, himself abiding in heaven. Because of who God is "all the works of the Lord" should bless him. We can identify with the three young men in the fiery furnace, remembering that God has saved us from countless perils. This canticle in particular tells us to fix our eyes on God, contemplating his wondrous nature. To some extent we forget ourselves as we engage in the one activity of praising God.

Psalm 150

In the canticle we learned how "blessed" God is in many ways. We contemplated his majesty and glory, recalling his power and dwelling in heaven. Now that we know who God is, we are called on to "praise" him. We are to attach praise to the place where God dwells and also to a range of God's attributes. Thus we hear of his "holy place" and "his mighty heavens." We think of his "powerful deeds" and "surpassing greatness." We are to take all musical instruments and to dance before the Lord. In one joyous singing with "trumpet," "lute," "harp," "timbrel," "strings," "pipes," and "cymbals," we summon all of creation to join in our praise.

Reading: Ezekiel 36:25-27

In this reading taken from the visions of the prophet Ezekiel, we hear of God's promise of redemption for human beings. What Christian references we can see in this passage! "I will sprinkle clean water upon you to cleanse you from all your impurities." Here we find the grace of baptism described: we are washed from all our sins. The action of God also goes deep. We all have "idols" to which we are attached. Each of us can easily make a list of created things to which we ascribe excessive value. But none of those is God, and if we allow ourselves to honor them above God, we have made them into "idols."

When God has washed away our sins and removed our idols, he goes deeper still. He will replace our hearts, made of stone, with hearts of flesh. Clearly he is going to make us into people who can love. But this will be possible only if we have, at the same time, a "new spirit." Once again, in Christian terms, we find a reference to the Holy Spirit. When the Holy Spirit lives in our hearts, we love both God and neighbor. When the Holy Spirit came on Pentecost, it transformed the apostles (Acts 2:1-21). We receive the same spirit in confirmation and are gradually transformed by its presence. God tells us then that the "new spirit" he will give us is his "spirit." With this spirit in our hearts, we will be able to lead holy lives.

This passage can be read as a description of baptism and confirmation and their effects. We rejoice greatly at what God has done for us. These lines from Ezekiel can also be read as a description of God's ongoing action. God is unchanging and his actions remain the same. Always, ever, he is cleansing us from our "impurities." Again and again we can go to confession and be cleansed. He is always renewing our inner nature. He keeps replenishing our hearts, making us ever more able to love. He ever gives us his Holy Spirit to live within us and to direct our lives. Our whole life is a gradual transformation in and by grace. God will be always faithful as he gives us his "Spirit in our hearts" (2 Corinthians 1:22) and forms Christ within us (Galatians 4:19).

Monday

Psalm 42

As we begin our day, we express our deep longing for God. We speak in direct address to God. We can hear in these lines our own voice and that of the Church. Like a deer that is desperately thirsty for water, I yearn for you, God. What I am thirsty for is God who gives me life. But I do not find him. My grief is very great and others likewise ask: "Where is your God?" Then I recall times of consolation when God was near. I can recall glad times of shared worship with others "wild with joy."

I speak to my own soul asking why it is disconsolate. I give it a command: "hope in God!" God is our savior and will bring us salvation. The psalmist explains the sadness of his soul in terms of his longing for his home and places of worship. I remember times of joyful worship. But all is different in my soul. Deep within my soul I experience only suffering as though I were drowning in sorrow. I feel swept away by God's "waves" and "torrents." But I will hold firm and discover that God loves me. "By day" I find his "loving kindness." By night I find cause to praise him with joy.

God is "my rock," my security. When he seems to be absent, I will cry out to him. My suffering is intensified by others too who ask me, "Where is your God?" My refrain will be the same: my hope is in God and it is he whom I will praise.

In this psalm we can hear the voice of Jesus during the passion. We can imagine how he longed for God as he carried his cross amid jeers and insults. In his suffering how he must have yearned for God like a "deer that yearns for running streams." In Gethsemane he wept at the thought of all the sins of all the ages he would have to bear. Then he may have recalled times and places of joyful worship. But in the psalm we hear the soul of Jesus proclaiming the right answer: hope in God and praise him. During his life Jesus experienced the "loving kindness" of the Father and had cause to praise him during nights of prayer. But in the passion the "torrents" and "waves" of sorrow swept over Jesus, and for a brief, terrible moment he lost the Father: "My God, my God, why have you forsaken me?" (Matthew 27:46). All around him were the cries of the crowd asking for a sign of God's favor to him. Yet in his soul Jesus kept hope and in the end committed his soul into the Father's care (Luke 23:46). Saying the psalm thus with Jesus, we enter deeply into both his sufferings and his faith.

From a Carmelite perspective this psalm speaks to us of the darkness and emptiness that forms part of our spiritual journey to God at the center of our souls. From self we must detach, and often the result is a sense of emptiness and loss. In this experience we may appear to lose God. We must learn to walk in faith alone. In such a state we yearn for God. We want desperately to enter into his presence within. We suffer grief as others too notice that we have lost our God. And then—how we remember times of consolation! But the answer is ever the same: hope and praise! We may find within that we have been drowned in sorrow and pain. But we trust in God's "loving kindness." Even in our "night" we will find cause to praise. No matter how terrible the suffering, no matter if we seem totally forgotten, the answer is ever to trust in God's saving power. God is at the center of our soul and is drawing us inward. The journey is long but the goal is sure.

Canticle: Sirach 36:1-5,10-13

In these lines we cry out in direct address to God in our own voice and especially in that of the Church, the new Jerusalem, the new Israel. As we thirsted for God in our first psalm of the morning, now we summon God to manifest himself to us and to give us his aid. We wish

God to reveal himself so that his "holiness" and "glory" might be recognized by others. We, as the new Israel, wish God's mercy. We ask for his "pity" on Jerusalem. We are that Jerusalem and long to be filled with God's "majesty" and "glory."

From a Carmelite perspective, we can read all of this canticle in a meaningful way. The calls for God to punish "unbelievers" can be seen as directed against negative inclinations within our own souls. We ask the "God of the universe," who miraculously abides in our own souls, to show himself, that is, to infuse our beings with his presence. If God makes his presence known, all within us will recognize who he is. Surely, then, there will be "signs" and "wonders" in our being as God's healing power and splendor are at work. Our soul is the new Israel, the new Jerusalem. We ask for "mercy" and "pity" on this soul. Our longing is for God to fill us with his "majesty." We are the "temple" of God; we can be filled with his "glory!"

Psalm 19A

In this splendid psalm our eyes are drawn upward to gaze at the glories of the heavens. What we are to see there is the "work" of God. We are filled with astonishment at the splendors we behold in the skies, a panorama of ever-changing beauty. The heavens tell an unending tale of wonder. So, the psalmist says, day and night keep telling this "story" which has one theme only: the glory of God.

But what kind of story is this? First of all, it is a silent story. We hear "no speech, no word, no voice." Second, night and day adopt a different form of "words" that extend through the whole universe. These "words" are their constant proclamation of the silent splendor of God. We then focus our attention on one particular wonder in the heavens: the sun. Eagerly it rises into the sky, rejoicing "like a champion to run its course." This sun starts in the east and covers the whole sky before it rests again. Its light and heat touch everything in the earth.

From a Carmelite perspective, we may adopt the approach of Elizabeth of the Trinity (described in the Introduction). The "heavens" can be taken as a reference to our own souls where God dwells. These souls, then, proclaim and should proclaim the "glory of God." Inwardly and through our whole being God makes his glorious presence known. We are ever a proclamation of the wonder of his works. This proclamation does not exist in the form of "speech" or "words" alone. It stems from God, living at the core of our being, suffusing us with his divine grace and love. In this soul there is also a light beyond all others. As the sun is to the sky, so Jesus is to the soul. He is the "bridegroom" of the Church. He is the Light that suffuses the soul and body. Nothing escapes the sight of Jesus as he loves us in our souls with an infinite love. How we welcome his presence! How we stand in awe at the splendid message of God's love that he proclaims!

Reading: Jeremiah 15:16

In this brief reading each of us can rejoice in a great truth: we bear the "name" of God. He has chosen us in baptism. As much as any prophet chosen of old, we are truly his. We hear too in this passage how we are to respond to the words of scripture. We are to "devour" them. They are to become our food and drink. If we hold firmly to such "words" and eagerly absorb them, we find that they are much, much more than simply words. They become the "joy and happiness" of our hearts. These words give us a share in the life of God and truly become for us the source of profound delight.

Tuesday

Psalm 43

In this psalm we address God directly. We can speak the psalm in our own voice and in that of the Church. As we begin the psalm, we are disconsolate. We feel threatened and attacked; we are in need of defense and rescue. We have made God our "stronghold" and yet we feel that he has rejected us because our foes oppress us. We do not understand. But we are sure of one thing: the "light" and "truth" of God can guide us. We ask for these. We want to go to one place only: the "holy mountain" where God dwells. If we can come there, then we will approach the "altar of God," the God who is the source of our "joy." And then too we will make music to God. Our souls are uplifted by hope and longing. We suddenly return to our present condition and circumstances, but, in light of the prayer we have uttered and the desire for God's presence we have expressed, we can now encourage our souls to have hope. We are determined to be faithful: yes, we will praise God with complete confidence and trust.

In this psalm we can hear the voice of Jesus during his passion. We can hear his plea for help when all cried: "crucify him" (Luke 23:21). As a human being, he experienced the sense of rejection by God when he cried out on the cross: "My God, my God, why have you forsaken me?" (Matthew 27:46). We can hear Jesus' prayer for "light" and "truth." We can feel his longing for the presence of God, the Father who was his "joy." In the midst of his sorrows, he held onto hope and was not disappointed.

In this psalm we can apply the Carmelite perspective. So often in our spiritual journey we feel abandoned and alone. Inwardly we encounter many weaknesses, faults, and failings from which we need rescue. We have made

God our "stronghold"; we firmly believe that he is at the center of our beings. Despite this, we experience sorrow; we feel "oppressed" by our own sinful natures. But hope dawns! From the core of our souls "light" can come and "truth." Those can guide us into the presence of God in our souls. Then, with what delight do we approach God! What thanks we proclaim! Even if now we feel sad and abandoned, we must cling to hope. God ever deserves our praise, endless praise. He will not fail us.

Canticle: Isaiah 38:10-14,17-20

In this canticle we hear the cries of a person who has been desperately ill. We can also hear our own voice as we recall perhaps times when we have been grievously sick. The speaker describes how death came close. Soon to be lost was the familiar world, relationships, life itself. The speaker refers to God as the actor in what is happening. God is like a weaver who is severing his threads. God is one who hands "over to torment." God is like a lion breaking bones. What is the condition of the speaker, crying "like a swallow" and moaning "like a dove?"

The speaker, despite all that is happening, keeps God in sight and cries out to him. Here there is no loss of faith. Here there may be no understanding of what is happening in this terrible suffering, but there is still trust. God is there in the pain. He is "surety."

Then the speaker utters lines of great joy. God preserved life and did so by forgiving all sins. God "cast behind" his back all these sins: in this location they are forgotten! Now, in thanksgiving, the speaker enthusiastically praises God. There is great cause for delight. The response that seems appropriate is to "sing . . . all the days of our life." God showed mercy and healed us. How can we ever thank him enough?

In this canticle, with great sorrow and compassion, we can hear of Jesus' sufferings during the passion. How young Jesus was at the time of his death! Surely he departed "in the noontime of life." He grieves that he will no longer "see the Lord . . . in the land of the living." He will have to leave his friends. Then we can hear with striking images how Jesus may have suffered on the cross. "You have folded up my life, like a weaver who severs the last thread." "You give me over to torment." "Like a lion" you break "all my bones." All of these sufferings the Father allowed for our sakes. We can also hear how Jesus describes himself: "I cry out"; "Like a swallow I utter shrill cries; I moan like a dove." We can perceive too how Jesus became weaker and weaker as he suffered: "My eyes grow weak, gazing heavenward."

Jesus calls on the Father to be his "surety." How truly he was! The Father raised Jesus from the dead, giving him life again. Truly, "the Lord is our savior." With Jesus, we proclaim with joy the "faithfulness" of the Father. We sing to him "all the days of our life."

Psalm 65

In this psalm of direct address, we speak to God in our own voice or in the voice of the Church. We begin by telling God that we owe him praise. The rest of the psalm then gives in rich profusion reasons that God deserves our praise. God hears "our prayer." God wipes away our "offenses," and only he can thus free us. We have access to God's "temple," and there he blesses us. God works "wonders" in our lives.

The whole world hopes in God. The psalmist now describes how God sustains the universe. He holds up "mountains." He stills the "roaring of the seas." Both east and west, "lands of sunrise and sunset," he fills with joy. God sends rain to make the earth fruitful. God's goodness causes the abundance of crops for human beings. Even "in the pastures of the wilderness" his "abundance flows." Wherever we look we see the working of God:

> The hills are girded with joy,
> the meadows covered with flocks,
> the valleys are decked with wheat.

So generous and great is God's generosity that all of these "shout for joy, yes, they sing."

Reading: 1 Thessalonians 5:4-5

Our dwelling as children of God is in the light. We are rightly called "children of light and of the day." We have nothing to do with "darkness" or "night." Because this is so, the "day" on which Jesus may return will never catch us "off guard." Jesus is the "true light" who came "into the world" (John 1:9). We who are the "light of the world" (Matthew 5:14) are akin to Jesus. We keep our eyes ever on him and thus we "belong" to the light.

Wednesday

Psalm 77

In this psalm we can hear our own voice and the voice of the Church as we cry out in pain and distress. In this psalm when we formulate questions about God, we describe him in the third person. When we wish to speak to God, we address him directly. The psalm is a form of meditation as we work carefully through the dilemma of losing any sense of God's presence. Sometimes in our lives God seems to be very present. Sweetly he pours consolations into our hearts, and faith and trust in his presence is easy. At other times, however, God seems far away. We look for and seek him, but we cannot find him. John of the Cross speaks profoundly of the "dark nights" through which we must pass on our spiritual journey. Teresa of Avila, likewise, speaks of the crushing absence of God on certain stages of our inner journey to him. Psalm 77 vividly describes how we feel at such a time. We ask questions. We make assessments. In each case we fail to understand what is happening to us. All we can do is cling to the faithfulness of God manifested in the past.

As Psalm 77 begins we "cry aloud to God" and we keep crying. We have been doing so by day and by night. We have lost God! Our souls refuse "to be consoled." At this time we cling tenaciously to our memories of earlier experiences of God. We cannot sleep; we are sorely troubled.

During this time questions arise from deep within our spirits. We attempt to interpret our experience. Is God rejecting us? Has he removed his favor? Has his love for us vanished? Are his promises no longer in effect? Has God forgotten mercy? Is he angry? Does he no longer show compassion? Our experience seems to tell us: God has changed! This seems especially to be the case because in the past God did such "mighty deeds" for us.

The psalmist then stops this kind of questioning. We may not grasp what is happening in our spiritual journey. God may seem to be distant, to be far from our lives. We may long intensely for his presence and seek him. But in faith we must hold firm. Thus we now address God directly, affirming what we know to be true of him. You, God, are holy. You, God, are great. You work wonders; you display your power to human beings; you redeemed us. In a most glorious moment in history you stirred the waters of the Red Sea and made a way for your people to escape from danger. When you acted thus to save your people, we saw wonders. The waters trembled; clouds "poured down rain"; the skies thundered; lightnings "flashed"; the earth was "moved."

In this experience of rescue, God was manifestly present. And yet God was not actually seen. The psalmist says: "Your way led them through the sea . . . and no one saw your footprints." He recalls that God after this led his people on their journey "by the hand of Moses and Aaron." These thoughts reassure us. God was present, but the Israelites did not see him. He can, when he chooses, make his presence very clear by signs and wonders. But often his guidance comes through others. God, however, is the shepherd who guides us "like a flock." We need not fear.

For the present, therefore, no matter what darkness may pervade our souls, no matter how distant God may seem, we must hold firm in faith. God is holy, and we can trust that his strength will save us in extreme distress. In the past we did not see his "footprints," but he was there. We are called, then, not to question his favor, love, mercy, or compassion. His promises are sure. Most of all, we are to recall that God's ways are "holy." In these we can place all our trust.

Canticle: 1 Samuel 2:1-10

These lines come from the Song of Hannah, rejoicing as she leaves the child Samuel in the temple for the Lord. It is a song of victory, the type of song that we may be able to sing once the experiences of Psalm 77 are over. It is a song that, as Christians, we can always sing because Jesus has risen from the dead. In this canticle we can hear our own voice and that of the Church.

We cry out with joy over our victory. We have overcome our enemies. The source of our triumph has been the Lord. He is holy. He is a Rock. This God is all-knowing. He has the role of judge. Because of this, it is not appropriate for human beings to boast.

How do we discern God's working in human affairs? We see many unexpected phenomena. The "mighty" are made weak; the "tottering," strong. The "well-fed" are hungry, but those without have an abundance. The childless woman has several sons, but the mother of many does not flourish.

The psalmist makes clear who God is. He controls life and death. He "makes poor" and "makes rich." He has the power to humble and to exalt. If we are needy, we can trust in God. He is able to raise the poor, put them among "nobles," and even make them into royalty. Such he did with David; such he can do again.

We learn the reasons that God's power is so great within our world. He founded our earth. As we live, we will find someone guarding us, if we are faithful. No hope awaits those who choose evil, not even if they are strong. Human beings "prevail" according to God's plan, not according to their "strength." It is God who "judges the ends of the earth." Our prayer is that his grace may be with us.

This Song of Hannah, as is well known, strongly influenced the Canticle of Mary (see below, Chapter 5). In both songs we encounter amazement at the way God works, a way so different from that of human beings. What is despised and ignored by the world God chooses and transforms into what is truly valuable. God is faithful from age to age and power belongs completely to him.

As Christians, as we read this Song of Hannah, we recall the triumph of Jesus. At the resurrection, the Father raised him to life, victorious over the real enemies whom we all face, sin and death. Jesus during his life on earth was "poor" and "needy," but now the Father has made "a glorious throne" his "heritage." Truly the Father has given "strength to his king," and exalted "the horn of his anointed." For our sake Jesus humbled himself (Philippians 2:7); now the Father has exalted him. Jesus is our model of conduct. No "arrogance" issued from his mouth. He teaches us how to be "faithful," tenderly guarded by a Father's care.

Psalm 97

This is a song of wondrous praise for God. We can sing it with our voice and in the voice of the Church. The kingship of God is our cause for rejoicing. God may be a hidden presence: "cloud and darkness are his raiment." But God is there and he rules the whole universe. We can be confident in him because his throne is "justice and right." The power of the Lord is amazing. We see his "fire" and "lightnings." At his presence "mountains melt." We behold his "justice" and his "glory." All those who believe in God can "rejoice" at the "judgments" of God that are revealed in the earth. The majesty of the Lord is beyond all description. What delights us most is that he loves us, guards us, and saves us. God is a "light" that breaks into our lives, bringing us "joy." We can endlessly "rejoice" in God. His "holy name" is ever glorious.

If we read this psalm from a Carmelite perspective, we can focus on God's presence within the soul. From this center he radiates his light throughout our whole being, bringing us "light" and "joy." We see God's complete power over all of our nature. Everything within us yields to his power. He is a hidden presence within, clothed in "cloud and darkness." Yet, when God's presence flows out from the center of our souls through the rest of our soul and all of our body, we are overwhelmed with gladness. We find in this God "justice and right" and love. We experience his protection; he saves us from our own sinfulness. How joyfully we praise his glorious presence within!

Reading: Romans 8:35, 37

In this brief passage we hear the question: "Who will separate us from the love of Christ?" The answer is essentially loud and clear: nothing! Paul imagines the kinds of things that could perhaps make us forget or

lose the love of Christ: "trial, or distress, or persecu-
tion, or hunger, or nakedness, or danger, or the sword."
In all of these hardships we might be tempted to ask:
Does Jesus still love us if this is happening to us? But
our conviction that Jesus does love us, our firm faith in
that love, transforms all these negative experiences. We
are not defeated or overwhelmed. Instead, we become
"more than conquerors because of him who has loved
us." The love of Jesus strengthens and makes us bold.
We come through triumphant! In the canticle we heard
Hannah describing God as making the weak strong. In
this passage of Romans we encounter the same message. God will be with his people in love, and all earthly
sufferings and hardships are transformed by that love.
We can ever be victorious because of the love of Christ.

Thursday

Psalm 80

We cry out to God in our voice and that of the Church
directly addressing him who is our "shepherd." This
psalm has a refrain that recurs three times: "God of
hosts, bring us back; let your face shine on us and we
shall be saved." The refrain suggests that we have wandered. The light of God's countenance, however, will
prove to be the source of our salvation. We begin the
psalm by asking God to shine his light on us and to
bring us his help. We utter the refrain as a cry for God's
mercy: at the moment, however, we do not feel God's
presence. Instead, we have "tears for . . . bread," "tears
for . . . drink." Our situation is one that allows others to
mock us. Once again we utter the refrain, more eagerly
now as we recall our sufferings.

We proceed to recall historical events, describing to
God how he once "brought a vine out of Egypt." God
delivered his people from bondage, and this "vine" flour-

ished. But now this vine is in trouble, "plucked . . . ravaged . . . devoured." Earnestly we ask God to come to "visit this vine" and to restore its fortunes. We remind him that the vine is his very own. We pray for strength. We then accept responsibility for what has happened to the vine: we have forsaken God. Life comes from God, and, filled with it, we will "call upon" his name. Now, with intensity and zeal, we repeat the refrain once again.

We can read this psalm from a Christian point of view. We identify with the sufferings that the Church undergoes. The Church is the "vine" that God has planted. It has spread widely, strong and flourishing. But it is also in trouble, desperately in need of God's protection. Jesus is the "man" God has chosen, the "man" to whom he has given "strength." Jesus is the "way and the truth and the life" (John 14:16). In him all can find salvation. We hope that God will help Jesus save us and save the nations. Under God's guidance the Church will walk in the right way. Filled with "life," it will offer worthy praise.

Canticle: Isaiah 12:1-6

In this canticle from Isaiah we can see a form of response to Psalm 80: God has answered! He has blessed us and we sing out our gratitude. In the first stanza we find ourselves addressing God directly. This direct address brings me very close to God. With joy I thank God who is now richly consoling me. In his presence I feel no fear. I feel even closer to God in the second stanza, especially if I place it too in direct address:

You, God, indeed *are* my savior;
I am confident and unafraid.
My strength and my courage *are you,* Lord,
and *you have* been my savior.

God has saved me. I am filled with confidence. God is "my strength and courage."

Isaiah then addresses us, telling us what will occur when we too find God as our savior. We also will feel joy as we "draw water at the fountain of salvation." We too will realize that we are saved. We are urged to express our gratitude with exuberance. The whole earth should know of his glorious achievements. We can be especially joyful because "great" in our midst is the "Holy One of Israel."

From the Christian point of view, we can hear in this passage the voice of Jesus from the third stanza to the end. In stanza three Isaiah speaks of drawing "water at the fountain of salvation." We recall Jesus telling the woman of Samaria that those to whom he gives "living water" will find within "a spring of water welling up to eternal life" (John 4:10, 14). In stanzas four to six, we can hear Jesus urge us to thank God, to make his deeds known, and to proclaim how marvelous he is to the whole world. All the earth should learn of the famous deeds of God. We can rejoice in particular because in our midst is the "Holy One of Israel." Jesus has revealed how close God is to us, dwelling in our very hearts.

Psalm 81

In Psalm 80 above, we cried out in great need to God. In this psalm, as in the canticle, we rejoice that God has saved us. Ever he has been our rescuer. In the first three stanzas the psalmist urges us to sing, shout, and play instruments in joy to God "our strength." We are to do so because God has urged us to act in this way. In the remaining six stanzas we hear the voice of God clarifying what his actions have been in helping us in the past.

God freed our heads and shoulders. We cried in distress and he saved us! God remained hidden "in the storm cloud." God also tested our fidelity in the past at Meribah. Then in the psalm we hear how God longs for us to honor him. He is the one who has rescued us! He wants to bless us: "Open wide your mouth and I will fill it." But we showed "stubbornness of heart." God respected our free will and left us to follow our "own designs." Again God tells us how he longs for us and how he would help us. We would find in him a complete defender. Most wonderful of all, he would "feed" us "with finest wheat" and fill us "with honey from the rock." Just as Moses sang of the way God gave Jacob "honey . . . from . . . rocks" and "products of its field" and "oil" (Deuteronomy 32:13), so in this psalm we hear of God's providential care. But all depends on our response. We are called on to be faithful. God must respect our free will. By rejecting him we have to walk on our own.

This psalm tells us very clearly of God's love for us. Read from a Christian point of view, it shows that this love is unfathomable. Though we remained disobedient and did not walk in his "ways," God sent us Jesus. He has overcome for us all our "enemies," the sins and failings that draw us on a wrong path. We opened wide our "mouth" and he filled it. He gave us the "finest wheat," Jesus, to be our living Bread in the Eucharist. However much, in "stubbornness of heart," we followed our own designs, he did not leave us in our sins. In the fullness of time he sent Jesus to save us. His plea to us is now, as it always is: be faithful. He will protect us and feed us abundantly, especially with spiritual food.

Reading: Romans 14:17-19

In this passage we hear of the essence of Christianity. We have within our hearts the Holy Spirit. His action is not to provide us with earthly food or drink. Instead, he gives us spiritual sustenance: justice, peace, and joy. Filled with these gifts of the Holy Spirit, we serve Jesus well. We please the Father and love our neighbor. Our aim, therefore, is "to work for peace" and "to strengthen one another."

Friday

Psalm 51

See discussion at *Week I, Friday, Morning Prayer,* p. 41

Canticle: Habakkuk 3:2-4, 13a, 15-19

In this canticle Habakkuk recalls God's actions in the past, especially the way in which he saved the Israelites at the Red Sea. This prophet calls on God to be compassionate. God comes from "Teman . . . from Mount Paran," both mountains to the south and west of Judah. What is God like? "His splendor spreads like the light" as he hastens to save his anointed people, the Israelites.

The prophet is filled with amazement and awe at the powerful presence of God. He confidently believes that his enemies will fall. In the final three stanzas we find a resounding call for us to trust in God, even though all around us seems to be crumbling and in ruin. Habakkuk says that, although all crops fail—fig, fruit, olive—and although all herds and flocks disappear, we are to "rejoice in the Lord" and "exult in *our* saving God."

The truth is: "God is *our* strength." What does he do for us? "He makes *our* feet swift as those of hinds and enables *us* to go upon the heights." This image is a striking one: God takes us to the very heights and allows us to have a commanding view of our world. The climb may be difficult. Often the heights may be hidden and obscure. But, if we trust, we can be sure of our destination. We will not be able to go to the heights on our own: God will take us there. As the first part of the canticle showed us, God can appear in great splendor. We can trust that he is ever with us and will bring us to triumph in the end.

Psalm 147:12-20

In this second part of Psalm 147 we are called on to praise God. We consider many of his actions, praying in our own voice and that of the Church. This psalm becomes most meaningful if the final four stanzas are changed to direct address.

> *You have* strengthened the bars of *our* gates,
> *you have* blessed the children within *us*.
> *You* established peace on *our* borders.
> *you* feed *us* with finest wheat.

In these lines we encounter the protection that God gives. He gives us peace and sustains us, providing "finest wheat."

> *You send* out *your* word to the earth
> and swiftly runs *your* command.
> *You shower* down snow white as wool,
> *you scatter* hoar-frost like ashes.
>
> *You hurl* down hailstones like crumbs.
> The waters are frozen at *your* touch;
> *you send* forth *your* word and it melts them:
> at the breath of *your* mouth the waters flow.

In these two stanzas we encounter the creative and sustaining action of God. What he says or commands is done. We see his guidance of nature. In winter his command is for "snow," "hoar-frost" and "hail-stones." Waters become frozen and still. In spring a new command goes forth: the ice melts and "the waters flow."

> *You make your* word known to Jacob,
> to Israel *your* laws and decrees.
> *You have* not dealt thus with other nations;
> *you have* not taught them *your* decrees.

God speaks and brings about all the changes in nature. He speaks in a special way to Jacob and Israel, declaring his "laws and decrees." They are privileged in being the receivers of a share in God's life expressed in his "laws" and "decrees."

If we read this psalm from a Christian point of view, we can interpret some lines as referring to Jesus. Thus when God "feeds *us* with finest wheat," we can think of Jesus and his wondrous presence in the Eucharist. When we twice hear of God sending forth "his word," we know that the reference is to God's creative presence in nature. But we can also recall that Jesus is the "Word" of God through whom "the world came to be" (John 1:10). "In him were created all things in heaven and on earth, / the visible and the invisible / . . . all things were created through him and for him" (Colossians 1:16). When we hear of God making known "his word," once again we may think of Jesus sent by the Father to teach and save us. "Through him *God was pleased* to reconcile all things for him, / making peace by the blood of his cross / . . . whether those on earth or those in heaven" (Colossians 1:20). We are the new "Jacob" and "Israel," and it is to us that God has sent his Son, his "Word," for our salvation.

Reading: Ephesians 2:13-16

In this passage we learn that the strong division between Jew and Gentile has been totally removed by the crucifixion of Jesus. His blood has brought us all together. Jesus is our "peace." He has reconciled all divergent groups, removing all hostility. He has removed as well "the law with its commands and precepts." Paul suggests that this law has been replaced by "one new man," i.e., humanity. He refers to all of us, now acting under the inspiration of grace and the Holy Spirit. What Jesus did on the cross was to "put to . . . death" all the "hostility" between different human groups. By his death, he made a new humanity. This is the Church, united in "peace" by Jesus and forming his mystical body.

Saturday

Psalm 92

In this psalm of direct address to God, we can sing in our own voice and that of the Church. We tell God that "it is good" to thank him, sing to him, and appreciate his love and truth at all times. Why? Because his deeds bring "joy" and his works are "great." And yet we do not easily understand what God does: his "designs" are "deep."

Never do we have to fear those who do evil because in the end evil will not thrive. Even if evil seems to abound "like grass," its existence is limited. In contrast, God abides forever. The psalmist now describes how God treats him. God gives the "strength" of a "wild-ox." He anoints with "purest oil." He makes the just "flourish" "like the palm tree and grow like a Lebanon cedar." Thus God infuses us with vigorous life; we are graced with strength and purity.

We then learn about this life that God gives to the just. They will be "planted in the house of the Lord." They will keep "bearing fruit," remaining "full of sap" and "green." Their message for others will be: "The Lord is just." In God there is "no wrong." He is our "rock."

God shares his life with those who are just. God himself is just. He rewards the just with a vibrant and productive life, a life that brings blessings ("fruit") to others. They dwell in the finest place, the "courts" of the Lord. For them God is a firm foundation and protection: he is "rock."

Canticle: Deuteronomy 32:1-12

These lines come from the "Song of Moses," a canticle of joyful praise to God for his love of his people. The song begins with a call to the "heavens" and the "earth" to listen. The contents of the song are to be like abundant "rain," "dew," "downpour" and "shower" upon a thirsty ground. The subject of the song—the greatness and renown of God—explains why all the universe should listen. Its contents resemble the richness of its subject. Who is God? A "rock," "faultless" and "right" in action. He is "faithful," "just," "upright," and free from "deceit."

The next stanza looks at the human race and its response to God. We are God's children: he is our "father" who "created" and "established" us. Yet we have proved "degenerate," "perverse," and "crooked." How "foolish" and "stupid" we have shown ourselves! If we remember the past, we should keep one thing in mind: Jacob and Israel were especially loved by God.

What care God has shown to us! In the next two stanzas we can use direct address, making the lines especially rich in meaning:

> *You* found *us* in a wilderness,
> a wasteland of howling desert.
> *You* shielded *us* and cared for *us*,
> guarding *us* as the apple of *your* eye.

> As an eagle incites its nestlings forth
> by hovering over its brood,
> so *you* spread *your* wings to receive *us*
> and bore *us* up on *your* pinions.
> *You, Lord,* alone *were our* leader,
> no strange god was with *us*.

The canticle describes God as our savior. He seeks us out as we wander in the desert. He shields us and cares for us, as his very special possession, the "apple of his eye."

Then God acts like an eagle teaching its young to fly. He urges us forth to try our wings. He hovers over us; he swoops under if we fall, catches us on his wings, and bears us to safety. Only God has been our "leader."

If we read this canticle from a Christian point of view, we see the wondrous care of the human race. God has been ever "faithful," saving not only Israel of old but all people. We have all sinned and proved ourselves unworthy, but God's response has been consistently generous. We, the Church, are the new Jacob, the new Israel. God found us in the wilderness of our sins and made us his precious and valued treasure. We have all become the "apple of his eye." God urges us on to new life, new enterprises. He does so like an eagle, teaching us to fly and rescuing us from falling. He alone is our leader. What love and devotion this God shows! Truly it is like "rain," "dew," "downpour" and "shower." How we long for all people to hear!

Psalm 8

In this psalm we stand in awe at God's creation and the place within it that he has assigned to human beings. As we gaze at the "earth," we are astounded at the presence of God that infuses it. The praise of God rises "above the heavens." The simple, the childlike— "children and . . . babes"—recognize God's majesty and cry it forth. Such praise puts to silence those who fail to honor or recognize God.

We now look upward and are more astonished still: "heavens . . . moon . . . stars," what glory they announce! The psalmist then turns his glance to human beings. How can God care for us so deeply? Yet he does, giving us an exalted position in creation. We have "glory and honor"; we have "power" over God's "works." "All things" are under our "feet." Those things include animals, birds, and fish. We end the psalm by repeating the opening lines: "How great is your name, O Lord our God, through all the earth!"

We can repeat this psalm in our own voice and that of the Church. We can also apply the psalm to Jesus as we find happening in Ephesians 1:22 where Paul says that the Father "has put all things beneath his feet," making him the "head" of the Church. In 1 Corinthians 15:24-28 once again we hear that God "has put all his enemies under his feet": Jesus is Lord of all. In Hebrews 2:5-9 we learn that redemption came through a human being, Jesus, and not through angels. Jesus, being God and man, has brought the human race "glory and honor." We are filled with endless praise and thanksgiving for this unwarranted gift of salvation.

Reading: Romans 12:14-16a

In these lines we find the challenge of Christianity. We are called on to "bless" those who hurt us. Our natural response would be to "curse." Grace allows us to "bless." We are to join closely with others in their particular experiences, rejoicing and grieving with them as circumstances require. We are to have one attitude for all people: love. Something can harm us: ambition that nurtures the self. If we associate with the lowly, we will find it easier to love.

II: Evening Prayer

Sunday, Evening Prayer I

Psalm 119:105-112

In this psalm we can first of all hear two voices, that of our own and that of the Church. As we anticipate Sunday, our day of rest, we tell God how highly we value his word. We address God directly, telling him of our desires and sufferings. God's word is "a lamp for my steps and a light for my path." The image here is a striking one. We are to imagine ourselves as being completely in darkness. We do not know which way to go; we cannot even see a path. Then a light appears! It is the word of God.

I tell God that I have resolved to follow his commands. My will, therefore, I wish to submit to God's way. At the present time "I am deeply afflicted." Now I realize that God's word can be life-giving and I pray that this be so. I want to know God and to learn from him. In the face of danger and attacks from enemies, the word of

God becomes a strong defense. Even more, I discover that God's will is something lasting: "my heritage for ever." Conforming to God's will, I find happiness. This will is the "joy" of my heart. My intention is to "carry out" this will fully in my life.

We can hear in this psalm also the voice of Jesus praying to the Father. We can envision him learning this psalm and expressing his delight with God's word. Clearly Jesus in his life on earth perfectly fulfilled the words of this psalm. For him God's word was a "lamp" and a "light." He ever obeyed the Father. During all times of suffering, Jesus "remembered" God's law. Truly the Father's will was his "heritage," the "joy" of his heart. Jesus in his life carried out God's will "in fullness." As he was during his earthly life, so Jesus is forever, both in heaven and living in our hearts. As we envision his response, we learn ourselves how to respond to God who directs our lives.

Psalm 16

In this wonderful psalm we address God directly. On one level we can speak the psalm in our own voice or in the voice of the Church. I ask God to keep me safe since I take refuge in him. My words to God are: "You are my God. My happiness lies in you alone." One of God's gifts to me is the love I feel for those who likewise honor him. I know that those who travel a different road will "increase their sorrows."

For me God is "my portion and cup." This image suggests that God is truly my food and drink. He is also my "prize": he is the object of my striving. He is the goal of my endeavors. I trust in God. His "lot" for me is to believe in him: how welcome this "heritage" to be a believer. There is no time when God is not with me. At night he "directs my heart." During the day I keep God "ever in my sight." With him "at my right hand, I shall stand firm."

Because I believe in God I am filled with joy: "My heart rejoices, my soul is glad." Nor do I fear death: my soul will go to God. To what do I look forward? "You will show me the path of life, the fullness of joy in your presence, at your right hand happiness for ever."

On another level in this psalm we can hear the voice of Jesus as he speaks to his Father. How true of Jesus to suppose that he would say to his Father: "You are my God. My happiness lies in you alone." Jesus loves deeply "the faithful ones who dwell in his land." For Jesus, the Father was "portion and cup"; he was "prize." Jesus rejoiced at both his "lot" and his "heritage." Jesus spent nights in prayer to the Father, who counseled him and directed his "heart." Jesus never took his eyes off the Father: he ever stood "firm."

In the next stanza of this psalm we can find, as Peter (Acts 2:25-31) and Paul (Acts 13:35) did, a reference to the resurrection:

> And so my heart rejoices, my soul is glad;
> even my body shall rest in safety.
> For you will not leave my soul among the dead,
> nor let your beloved now decay.

The Father saved Jesus from death. The last stanza shows us Jesus ascended into heaven:

> You will show me the path of life,
> the fullness of joy in your presence,
> at your right hand happiness for ever.

If we adopt a Carmelite perspective, this psalm becomes a source of profound prayer. Addressing God within my soul, I say, "Preserve me, God, I take refuge in you. *Truly* you are my God; *truly you are* my happiness." My choice is God. I will not make any creature or created thing into a god, for this is a way to grief. God dwelling at the center of my being is "my portion and cup" and also "my prize." To know that I live with God in my soul makes my "lot" delightful. What other "heritage" could I desire?

This wondrous God in my soul "gives me counsel" at night. Then too he "directs my heart." When I am awake, I focus on God within. In his presence I "stand firm." My response to who God is within my very being is one of great joy. Truly "my soul is glad." I do not fear death since God will take my soul to himself. Just as I find delight in God's presence in my soul here on earth, I can hope for "the fullness of joy in his presence" and "happiness" with God forever.

Canticle: Philippians 2:6-11

See discussion at *Week I, Sunday, Evening Prayer I,* p. 51.

Reading: Colossians 1:2b-6a

Paul prays that we may have "grace and peace." He praises two things: "faith in Christ Jesus" and "love" for other people. He suggests that both of these rest on the "hope" awaiting us in heaven. Where did this "hope" come from? The "gospel." The fruit of this gospel is love. This "gospel" will continue to grow "everywhere in the world." This passage thus encourages us to have "faith," "hope," and "love," all fruits of the gospel and all precious gifts of the Father.

Sunday, Evening Prayer II

Psalm 110:1-5, 7

See discussion at *Week I, Sunday, Evening Prayer II,* p. 52.

Psalm 115

In this psalm we are called on to put our trust in God who abides in heaven. Correctly and truthfully all glory belongs to the name of God, and we ask him to glorify this name. "Not to us" should glory come but to God. This God is not like the idols that others may worship. God, the source of "love and truth," is a living God who dwells "in the heavens." This God is free, doing "whatever he wills." We delight in the will of God because we believe in his "love and . . . truth."

Because God is who he is, we should trust him. Ever to human beings God is a "help" and a "shield." God remembers all people and will bless all of us, whether we are "little" or "great." The location of these blessings will be the earth that God has given to human beings. God dwells in heaven but showers his blessings upon us. Our appropriate response will be to bless this wondrous God "now and for ever."

We do not hear our voice in this psalm directly addressing God. We listen to the psalmist as a teacher who tells us about God and his ways. We are called on to bless this God whom we can trust and who will bless us. We long for God's name to be glorified since all glory belongs justly to him. We delight in hearing that God has given us the earth and that he will help and protect us.

Canticle: Revelation 19:1-7

See discussion at Week I, Sunday, Evening Prayer II, p. 55.

Reading: 2 Thessalonians 2:13-14

In these lines Paul describes all Christians as those "chosen for salvation." We are to show "holiness of spirit" and "fidelity to truth." What we can hope for is "the glory of our Lord Jesus Christ." As we end our day of rest, we can rejoice in the abounding and overwhelming wonder of God's call to each of us. Truly for this call we can never be too grateful.

Monday

Psalm 45–I

From a Christian point of view we find in this psalm a splendid picture of Jesus as our king. We hear our own voice and the voice of the Church. We address our "king" directly, describing who he is. As we begin the psalm, we feel the love that wells up in our hearts for Jesus. The words pour forth swiftly, our "tongue as nimble as the pen of a scribe." How fitting our description of Jesus:

> You are the fairest of the children of men
> and graciousness is poured upon your lips:
> because God has blessed you for evermore.

We long to see the message of Jesus triumphant throughout the world. Jesus deserves to "ride on in triumph" because, for us, he has conquered sin and death. Truly the cause of Jesus is one of "truth," "goodness," and "right." Jesus will overcome all evil. We turn to God and describe his power: his throne "shall endure for ever." Most importantly, God's reign is one of "justice." We rejoice that we can ever trust this God.

We speak then again of Jesus as the Messiah. Jesus loves "justice"; he hates "evil." Because he acts in these ways, God "has anointed" Jesus with the "oil of gladness" beyond all other rulers. Jesus is truly the "Christ," the anointed one, beloved and chosen by the Father. Such a king is rightly loved by "daughters of kings." Rightly beside him stands a "queen in gold of Ophir." In these references we can think of all those who have, under religious vows, chosen to follow Christ. We can think too of one woman in particular, Mary, rightly standing as a "queen" beside her Son.

If we read this portion of Psalm 45 from a Carmelite perspective, we acclaim the presence of Jesus in our soul. He is the Bridegroom of every soul, and our hearts can never love him enough. Words pour forth as we greet within "the fairest of all the children of men." We encounter one gracious in speech, strong in the victory of the resurrection, defender of "truth and goodness and right." We are eager that Jesus overcome in our beings anything that is at odds with him. We wish to be all his. We remember the Father and the everlasting nature of his kingdom. Jesus is favored because he ever loves "justice" and hates "evil." Within our souls Jesus is the chosen, the anointed one. He is a sweet fragrance to our beings. Our soul is a "palace" that greets Jesus with "music." Our soul is a daughter of a king and a "queen" that bestows all its love on Jesus. He, the king, deserves all the love of our hearts.

Psalm 45–II

In part two of Psalm 45 we turn our attention to the bride who is attracted to the king. He is so worthy to be loved! If we make God our first priority and love him, he will bless us. He deserves all of our devotion. The psalmist tells a "daughter": "Forget your own people and your father's house." Then she will rightly be chosen by the king and serve him alone. If she makes him her choice, she will be honored and "clothed with splendor." Robed magnificently, she will enter the palace of the king, accompanied by "maiden companions." "Amid gladness and joy" they will enter "the palace of the king." The marriage of the bride and the king will be fruitful. For the bride, her children will become her new family, strong and flourishing.

This part two of Psalm 45 can also be read from a Carmelite perspective. How appropriate these lines for all souls who have consecrated their lives under religious vows! We can address our soul as "daughter" and urge it to "forget" everything and everyone except Jesus who dwells as a Divine Guest at its center. When the soul has eyes only for Jesus, it becomes truly beautiful.

It can give all its devotion to him. Within our souls we can turn our attention in many directions. We can also, with our wills, strive to focus on Jesus alone. In a way it is our wills that can enter his presence. When the will does this, it is "clothed with splendor." Joyously, gladly, it enters the "palace of the king," the holy and wondrous presence of Jesus. There it will, enrapt in the divine radiance of Jesus, produce much fruit in love. Such fruit is worthy of praise.

Canticle: Ephesians 1:3-10

See discussion at *Week I, Monday, Evening Prayer,* p. 58.

Reading: 1 Thessalonians 2:13

Paul describes the proper way for us to receive the Good News. It is the "word of God," not merely human talk. It is also a power at work in us if we believe. Scripture, inspired by the Holy Spirit, transforms us, making us ever more like Jesus. Truly these truths are a cause for thanksgiving!

Tuesday

Psalm 49–I

In this psalm we find an answer to a question that may occur to all of us: why is it that people with vast wealth seem able to act with malice and cruelty and pay no penalty? The psalmist begins by calling on all of us to listen to his "wisdom" and "insight." He answers the question posed above by observing that wealth cannot buy "life." One cannot give God money to ensure that we live on. All must die. We also cannot purchase "the ransom" of our soul. It is the human condition for all to perish, leaving their wealth to others. Instead of hope of eternal life, these rich people have their graves as "their homes for ever." Riches blind people and remove the possibility of wisdom. Such individuals become no better than "beasts that are destroyed."

In the Christian context we can learn much from this psalm. "Wisdom" is not something that we can purchase. Worldly riches can prove harmful because they distort our thinking. They can also give a false sense of power so that we imagine that we can do anything. But money has no positive effect on the soul, only a potentially negative one. Jesus has warned us of the difficulty that the rich person faces in getting into heaven. "It is easier for a camel to pass through the eye of a needle than for one who is rich to enter the kingdom of God," he tells us (Matthew 19:24). He urges us to place the highest value on our souls. In this we will prove wise. Valuing wealth leads us to foolish returns. We lose our perspective on what is of true worth.

Psalm 49–II

The psalm proceeds to describe the fate of those who set their hearts on money. They seem to be powerful: they "have others at their beck and call." The end they face will be most undesirable, and then all "their outward show vanishes." Instead of wisdom truly enriching the soul, what those people have is only a superficial glitter, soon to perish.

For us who love God and make him the focus of our lives, hope is strong. God will "ransom" us from death and take our souls "to himself." We have no cause for envy of those who are rich: their "glory" is short-lived. The praises of others prove to be an empty gift, no replacement at all for the life of the soul. Truly in our attitude to riches we can be sorely tempted. We may easily come to lack "wisdom" and resemble "the beasts that are destroyed." The antiphon that attends this psalm in the *Hours* succinctly teaches us the perspective to have. "Store up for yourselves treasure in heaven, says the Lord."

Canticle: Revelation 4:11; 5:9,10,12

See discussion at *Week I, Tuesday, Evening Prayer,* p. 61.

Reading: Romans 3:23-25a

This reading sums up the whole Christian message. Paul suggests that all people had a chance to share in the "glory of God." But we all "have sinned." Without any claims that we can justly make, God justified us by a wondrous gift. He did so through the actions of Jesus whose blood has made expiation for all those who believe in him. God is just: all sin requires atonement. But God, in an act of indescribable generosity, achieved this atonement through the death of his own Son. God has made us free! What has happened is an entirely free gift.

Wednesday

Psalm 62

In this psalm we pray peacefully and quietly in our own voice and in that of the Church. This is a psalm in which the altering of some lines to direct address proves to be very helpful.

> In *you, God,* alone is my soul at rest;
> my help comes from *you.*
> *You* alone *are* my rock, my stronghold,
> my fortress: I stand firm.

In these lines I perceive the one place where I can be truly "at rest" and at peace: in God. When I am thus resting in God, I find a great source of strength. God helps me. What is God for me: "rock . . . stronghold . . . fortress"? All these images imply firmness and solidity. Resting in God who is thus, "I stand firm."

Now I gaze at what is happening around me. The psalmist describes people attacking viciously as though I were something fragile, a "tottering wall" or a "tumbling fence." How different I appear from God who is "rock . . . stronghold . . . fortress!" My enemies want to destroy me. They lie. They appear to be friends but are really enemies. In light of those hostile forces I make a prayer:

In *you, God, may my soul be at rest;*
for my hope comes from *you.*
You alone *are* my rock, my stronghold,
my fortress: I stand firm.

I now pray that what I knew in the first stanza I will put into effect. I will withdraw into God as my place of rest. I expand on what I have already grasped and say more:

In *you, God,* is my safety and glory,
the rock of my strength.

No matter what dangers I encounter, I will find salvation in God. He will be my "strength"; he will ensure my success.

As the psalm continues, I turn and urge other people to accept the truths that I have grasped. I tell them: "Take refuge in God"; "Trust him at all times." I urge them to do as I have done: "Pour out your hearts before him." Why? "God is our refuge." If we do this, we have no one to fear, either great or small.

We human beings face temptations. We could trust "oppression . . . plunder . . . riches." But placing our trust in such as these is foolish. What we know about God are two essential truths: he has power and he has love. Speaking directly to God, we say "you repay" all of us according to our deeds. If we trust God only, seek our rest and peace in him, and pour out our hearts to him, we can believe that he will repay us in a positive way for our "deeds." Truly we will experience his profound love for us. If we behave in this way, we do not need to fear others, no matter how cruel and heartless. God will likewise repay such people for their "deeds." For us God will remain: "rock . . . stronghold . . . fortress."

In this psalm we can also hear the voice of Jesus, especially at the time of his passion. Jesus finds rest only in the Father who is for him "rock . . . stronghold . . . fortress." The next two stanzas vividly describe what happened to Jesus during the crucifixion. He was like a "tottering wall" and a "tumbling fence." He, being "one man," was attacked to be broken down. He encountered human deceit and treachery. Then we can hear Jesus pray for his soul to find rest in God. He knows the Father is "safety and glory, the rock" of his strength. We can hear Jesus also urge us to take refuge in God, to trust him and to share all our sufferings with him. We are not to trust "oppression . . . plunder . . . riches." No, the Father has all power and he is love. We can firmly believe that he will treat us according to our actions. Such faith gives us hope and peace.

Psalm 67

In this psalm we address God in our voice and the voice of the Church. We are asking God for blessings. The psalm has a refrain that occurs twice in which we pray that all "peoples" will praise God. We begin in direct address: "O God, be gracious and bless us and let your face shed its light upon us." We wish to encounter in God a gentle, loving presence. We wish to receive "light" from him that will enlighten our lives. We then say that if God does bless us richly, others will come to know of his "ways" and will recognize his "saving help." We utter the refrain, praying that all peoples may know God. In the next stanza we pray further that the nations may be filled with joy at recognizing God's justice, fairness, and guidance. Once again we utter the refrain. In the last stanza we say that our prayer has been answered! God has blessed us with the fruits of the earth. We hope that he will continue to pour out blessings so that no one will fail to appreciate his goodness.

Canticle: Colossians 1:12-20

See discussion at *Week I, Wednesday, Evening Prayer,* p. 64.

Reading: 1 Peter 5:5b-7

Peter teaches us how to relate to other people. We are to come to them wearing a particular garment, that of humility. He quotes Proverbs 3:34 saying that God "is stern with the arrogant but to the humble he shows kindness." If we "bow" to God's control, it will be in his power to lift us high, should he wish to do so. To be in a high place on our own strength is foolish: we will encounter a "stern" God. Our lowliness allows God perfect freedom to do with us as he wishes. The last line of this reading brings us great consolation: "Cast all your cares on him because he cares for you." Psalm 62 had taught us that our rest is "in God alone" and that we should "pour out *our* hearts before him." Once again we hear the message: God "cares" for us. He wants to take our cares from us. We can boldly "cast" them on him! Thus we find the road to serenity and peace.

Thursday

Psalm 72–I

We read this psalm in two parts, hearing wondrous praise of the Messiah. We pray the psalm in our own voice and in the voice of the Church. It takes on particularly rich meaning if, from stanza two on, we change to direct address. From a Christian point of view, we are speaking of and to Jesus.

In stanza one we make our request to the Father: fill your king with "judgment" and "justice" so that he may judge "in justice" and "right judgment" those who are "poor." Here we can consider how Jesus will come again to judge all peoples. Those who are "poor," empty of self and freed from their sins, will benefit from the blessings of the "judgment" and "justice" he will display. We can rejoice that he comes to us in our poverty and need.

As we begin the next stanza, we pray that "peace" and "justice" may pervade the whole world. We can then address Jesus directly:

> May *you* defend the poor of the people
> and save the children of the needy
> and crush the oppressor.

All these things Jesus has accomplished: all "poor" and "needy" people have been saved. Our aggressor, Satan, has been crushed through the passion and death of Jesus.

> *You* shall endure like the sun and the moon
> from age to age.
> *You* shall descend like rain on the meadow,
> like raindrops on the earth.

Jesus has a reign that will never end. To every soul he brings abundant life, nurturing growth like the rain. When we are dry and in need of spiritual sustenance, Jesus comes, refreshing our souls with the sweet moisture of grace.

> In *your* days justice shall flourish
> and peace till the moon fails.
> *You* shall rule from sea to sea,
> from the Great River to earth's bounds.

Once again we hear that the effects of Jesus' reign will be "justice" and "peace." The whole world will be his domain, from the "Great River," the Euphrates, to "earth's bounds." To all nations the gospel will come, triumphantly spreading peace and justice.

In the next two stanzas we learn that all will honor Jesus. His "enemies," all sinfulness and death, will "fall." All earth's rulers will revere Jesus, falling "prostrate" before him. "All nations shall serve" Jesus, saved by his precious blood and enlivened in a new way by the Holy Spirit. Joyfully we serve, spreading Jesus' message of love and forgiveness.

Psalm 72–II

We now learn why the whole world will revere Jesus and be eager to serve him.

> For *you* shall save the poor when they cry
> And the needy who are helpless.
> *You* will have pity on the weak
> and save the lives of the poor.
> From oppression *you* will rescue their lives,
> to *you* their blood is dear.

Once again we hear of the "poor" and the "needy." Jesus comes to save those "who are helpless" and shows "pity on the weak." We are dear to Jesus. He recognizes how, in our frailty, we may be crushed by our own sins and the sins of others. We are the "helpless," the "weak," the "poor." In our distress we can call on one who will "save" us, Jesus, showing forth the very meaning of his name. To him we can flee in times of "oppression." We can be sure that our lives are "dear" to him.

As we finish this stanza we can say:

> Long may *you* live,
> may the gold of Sheba be given *you*.
> We shall pray for *you* without ceasing
> and bless *you* all the day.

Our hearts well up with joy at who Jesus is and what he has accomplished for us. We want him to receive all that the earth treasures. We "bless" him all day long. In our earthly journey he has brought us hope. He is there to love us when we are in distress. He transforms our days with joy.

In the next stanza we pray that abundance and prosperity will fill the whole earth. We hope that human beings may flourish "like grass on the earth." Jesus has brought our souls the abundant life of grace. This grace is his rain that waters our inner life and allows us to grow spiritually. With this grace operative within, we can truly "flourish" like the verdant "grass" that bedecks the earth.

Again our hearts leap with gladness as we think of Jesus and what he has done.

> May *your* name be blessed for ever
> and endure like the sun.
> Every tribe shall be blessed in *you,*
> all nations bless *your* name.

We want Jesus to reign through all time and to "endure like the sun." Jesus is the "light of the world" (John 8:12), truly a "sun" in our lives. He scatters the dark: we have been called "out of darkness into his wonderful light" (1 Peter 2:9). The gospel message is for all tribes and nations. All human beings will come to "bless" the name of Jesus. "At the name of Jesus / every knee should bend, / of those in heaven and on earth and under the earth, / and every tongue confess that / Jesus Christ is Lord, / to the glory of God the Father" (Philippians 2:10-11).

We end this psalm by blessing the Father.

> Blessed be *you,* Lord, God of Israel,
> who alone *work* wonders,
> ever blessed *your* glorious name.
> Let *your* glory fill the earth.
> Amen! Amen!

God alone "works wonders" for human beings, and the greatest wonder he gave us was his Son. We pray that God's name be "ever blessed" and that his "glory" might "fill the earth." The work of Jesus that brings about the salvation of all peoples most abundantly glorifies the Father. To this we cry aloud: "Amen! Amen!"

Canticle: Revelation 11:17-18; 12:10b-12a

See discussion at *Week I, Thursday, Evening Prayer,* p. 69.

Reading: 1 Peter 1:22-23

The goal of the Christian life is partly to love generously other people. Peter tells us that "obedience to the truth," the truth revealed in and by Jesus, has made such a love possible. Our purpose, therefore, is to love more and more, "constantly from the heart." We have been born anew from something planted in our hearts: "the living and enduring word of God." We have here a reference to Scripture as the source of teaching. We have also a reference to Jesus, the Word of God, "living," "enduring," who dwells within our hearts and makes us able to love.

Friday

Psalm 116:1-9

We speak this psalm in the first person, describing how God saved us from danger. Once again this psalm becomes very rich in meaning if we change to direct address.

> I love *you, Lord,* for *you* have heard
> the cry of my appeal;
> for *you* turned *your* ear to me
> in the day when I called *you.*

In this stanza I rejoice, telling God that he heard me when I sorely needed him. In the next stanza I recall that "death" and the "anguish of the tomb" threatened me. My response was to cry out: "O Lord my God, deliver me!"

How gracious *are you*, Lord, and just;
you, God, have compassion.
You, Lord, protect the simple hearts;
I was helpless so *you* saved me.

I ponder on who God is: "gracious" and "just." God is compassionate. What attracts God are "simple hearts." My helplessness drew God to save me. I address my soul with confident words, telling it to "rest." Why can I do this?

For *you, Lord, have* been good;
you have kept my soul from death,
my eyes from tears
and my feet from stumbling.

I will walk in *your presence, O Lord,*
in the land of the living.

God has saved my life. He has removed my cause for "tears." He keeps me "from stumbling." Now, with clear vision and firm steps, I can live in the "presence" of God, still sharing this world with others.

How you, Lord, have blessed me! You saved me from illness and sorrow! You loved me because I was helpless, having a "simple heart." How I love you in turn and in return!

From a Carmelite perspective we can hear the cry of the soul to God who dwells within. In the opening line we say how we "love" this God, for he listened when we cried out to him. What was my situation? "Sorrow" and "distress" filled my soul. I sought God to save me. He showed compassion. My heart was "simple," fixed solely on God at the center of my being and longing for him. No one could help me but only God, the Divine Guest of my soul. And God came to my aid.

I can now address my soul, urging it to be calm and peaceful. To it "the Lord has been good." My "sorrow" and "distress" are ended. As I live, I will be in the presence of God, who abides within. Here I can rest secure.

Psalm 121

In this very lovely psalm we place all our trust in God. We pray in our own voice and that of the Church. Truly, too, we can hear the voice of Jesus praying to the Father, praying for us, and telling us who God is. In the first stanza we have a question posed with its answer. I gaze upward seeking help. From where will it come? There is one source of help: "the Lord who made heaven and earth."

In the next stanza we hear a prayer expressed on our behalf: "May he never allow you to stumble!" We need not fear such an occurrence because "Israel's guard" neither "sleeps" nor "slumbers." Since God is awake, we will always be safe. He keeps us ever from stumbling.

In the next two stanzas we hear who God is. He is "guard" and "shade." He stays close to us. Nothing external, neither sun nor moon, can hurt us. God is especially protective, keeping us from evil, guarding our soul, guarding all of our movements.

From a Carmelite perspective we can turn our gaze inward and rejoice over what we discover. God dwells at the center of our souls. When I look for help, I find that it comes from God. This God at the core of my being is ever wakeful and watchful: he never "sleeps." Who is he within? A "guard," a "shade." He keeps careful and continuous watch over my soul. "Both now and for ever" he is the protection of my soul.

Canticle: Revelation 15:3-4

See discussion at *Week I, Friday, Evening Prayer,* p. 72.

Reading: 1 Corinthians 2:7-10a

In this passage we learn of the wondrous plan of God. "Before all ages" God planned the salvation of human beings, doing so in order that they might share in his "glory." The Gospel, the whole story of Jesus, his teachings, crucifixion, and resurrection, form "God's wisdom." This wisdom is a "hidden wisdom." It is not immediately apparent to eye or ear. If it had been, human beings would never have put Jesus, the "Lord of glory," to death. This wisdom covers what God has already done through the life and death of Jesus. It extends also into the future where it is likewise "hidden." Once again we can say that our eyes and ears have not perceived what awaits us.

Even more, it has not "so much as dawned" on us "what God has prepared for those who love him." We can imagine what this may be. We can hope for what it may include, but what will happen will exceed all our imaginations and hopes. We share now in the Gospel, "God's wisdom," and we do so "through the Spirit." Thus we rejoice in our salvation and in our hopes of future glory.

3.
Week III: Morning and Evening Prayer

What joy can ever compare with
the gentle touch of your hand?

I: Morning Prayer

Sunday

Psalm 93

We begin our day with praise of God, praying in our voice and the voice of the Church. In the first and fourth stanzas we refer to God in the third person. In the second, third, and fifth stanzas we address him directly. Who is the Lord? He is "king," robed with "might" and "power." We speak to God, so grateful that he has made the earth and his throne "firm." We need not fear because our dwelling place and the dwelling of God who rules us with love are not to be moved. Then we describe the essence of God: "from all eternity, O Lord, you are."

We speak of the "waters," probably representing forces of disorder or chaos. These "waters" appear to challenge God but to no avail. We describe God as "greater" than any "waters" or "surgings of the sea." Our God is "glorious on high." We speak confidently to God. We can trust his decrees. We know that he is holy.

This psalm confirms our confidence in God. We need not fear anything because he is stronger than all forces that could destroy us. We need not fear that the earth will be "moved" because God has made it "firm." We can trust the law, the "decrees," he lays out for us to follow. Most of all, we can ever revere God because "holiness" ever surrounds him.

Canticle: Daniel 3:57-88, 56

See discussion at *Week I, Sunday, Morning Prayer,* p. 23.

Psalm 148

In the canticle we heard all creation called on to praise God. In a similar way in this psalm we hear a call to praise God. We are to praise him everywhere. All creation is to join in this praise. First, we look up at the heavens and summon all these to utter praise: "angels," "sun," "moon," stars." Everything in this region obeys the laws set by God "which shall not pass away." Second, we gaze at the lower regions: earth and oceans and all they contain. All creatures—fish, animals, birds—are to join in our praise. Third, we call upon all human beings—young, old, lofty and lowly—to praise God.

Why should all creation utter such praise? God alone is "exalted." "Splendor" attends his "name." He strengthens his people. He "comes close" to his children. When he does so, their response is "praise." This psalm, which we can proclaim in our own voice and that of the Church, urges us to grasp the wondrous nature of the God who created the whole universe. This God does not stay at a distance. He comes close to strengthen us. How we rejoice in his love!

Reading: Ezekiel 37:12b-14

The scene of these lines is Babylon, during the exile. Ezekiel has just described the vivid coming-to-life of the "dry bones." Now he speaks of the "graves" from which the people will "rise." They will return from exile. God will fill his people with his "spirit." He has made a promise which he will fulfill without fail.

From a Christian perspective we can read this passage on two levels. First, Jesus has given us new life in baptism. We live by the Holy Spirit which he has poured into our hearts. We have found our homeland in the Church. Second, we look forward to the resurrection of the body. Yes, we shall "rise" from our graves when God opens them. Then we will dwell in our true homeland of heaven. God's love has ever been the same. He fills us with his own "spirit." He ever gives us new life.

Monday

Psalm 84

We sing this lively psalm in our own voice and that of the Church. We express our deep love for the place where God dwells, the place where we can go in joy to worship our God. Truly we say in gladness: "How lovely is your dwelling place, Lord, God of hosts." Our souls approach this dwelling with longing. We are delighted that we can enter therein. The "altars" of God provide a "home" and haven for "sparrow" and "swallow." How much more for us! Happy are those who dwell in God's house! Their constant activity is to praise.

This is who we are. Our happiness comes also from drawing strength from God. All our longing is to go to "Zion," the seat of God's temple. Even as we travel through hostile terrain, our inner joy and happiness transforms it. God responds likewise and pours down "rain" with its blessings. We receive grace upon grace. As we approach God's house, our "strength" becomes greater and greater.

We now address God directly, calling on him to hear our prayers. He is our shield: we ask him to gaze on us with love. We tell God: "One day within your courts is better than a thousand elsewhere." To be with God and God's people is a far greater delight than time in any other setting. The reason that this is so? God is "rampart" and "shield." He is, therefore, a sure defense. He also gives us many blessings: "favor and glory." If we strive to "walk without blame," he will greatly bless us. Our happiness comes from trusting God.

From a Carmelite perspective, this psalm resounds with rich meaning. Where is God's dwelling place? In the center of our souls. This abode is "lovely" because God is present. As I look inward, I yearn to be in God's presence. As I anticipate coming into this presence, my heart and soul "ring out their joy." I am like a "swallow" or "sparrow" in having a home in God: I can withdraw into the center of my soul and find him there.

Yes, when we find God within, all is joy. We ever sing God's praises. We are filled with strength from him. We may have to tread through a "Bitter Valley," but with the "springs" of joy coming from God's presence within, we transform the bitterness. We find that God also sends blessings and fills us with ever-increasing strength. As we choose to enter deep into the core of our being in prayer, we hope to come into God's very presence.

We address God directly, asking him to hear our prayer. Deep in peace and recollection, we know that this "one day" is better than any other could be anywhere. We find God within: "rampart" and "shield." We receive "favor" and "glory." Striving to be blameless in God's sight, we encounter his great goodness. To trust in this ever-present God is sheer happiness.

Canticle: Isaiah 2:2-5

This canticle describes what Jerusalem will be for the whole world. As Christians we see the Church as the New "Jerusalem," founded on the redeeming sacrifice of Jesus on the cross. The lines resound with a lofty image of what the Church will be for all peoples. This "mountain of the Lord's house" shall be the "highest mountain." All "nations" will come, yearning for this house of God. Here God will "instruct us in his ways" so that we can "walk in his paths." From this house will come "instruction" and the "word of the Lord." God will judge the nations and will bring peace to everyone. All signs of dissension—sword, spear, training for war—will disappear. Instead, we will cultivate activities of peace. If we walk in the light of God, this light will help to make us one.

From a Carmelite point of view we can see in this canticle a call to the center of our soul. Yes, let us go to God's "mountain," to his dwelling in our own being. All of us are called there. From within God will instruct us. Then we will be able to "walk in his paths." God will change us inwardly. All inclinations to violence will be replaced by yearnings for peace. We will be illumined from within.

Psalm 96

We sing this psalm in our own voice and in the voice of the Church, praising joyfully our wondrous God. From a Christian point of view we can see this psalm as a proclamation of Jesus, especially in the last stanza. The psalm calls for an open, exuberant response to the wondrous nature of God. What should our response be? "A new song" that blesses God. We mention these features of God: his "help," "glory," and "wonders." Why is the Lord "great and worthy of praise?" God created the world. With him we find "majesty," "state," "power," and "splendor."

The psalmist calls on us to honor God, recognizing his "glory and power." The whole "earth" is to worship him. God is creator. God is going to "judge the peoples in fairness." The whole of creation should acclaim this God with joy: "heavens," "earth," "sea," "land," "all the trees of the wood."

As we come to the final stanza, direct address leads us to focus our view on Jesus:

at the presence of the Lord for *you come,*
you come to rule the earth.

With justice *you* will rule the world,
you will judge the peoples with *your* truth.

Jesus has come to redeem the world, and at this we rejoice. He will come again. He will rule with justice and with truth. The resurrected Christ has taught us to long for his return. He will bring us his peace, filling us with love.

Reading: James 2:12-17

This brief reading emphasizes who we are as Christians. Jesus has set us free. With his gift of peace we can freely choose to do what is right. In our actions what matters most is mercy. This must be the foundation of all our relationships with others.

Tuesday

Psalm 85

We begin our morning prayer this Tuesday by praying in our own voice and that of the Church. We address God directly, calling out in distress. We say to God: in the past you "forgave" us, forgetting your "anger" at our sins. You "favored" us and "revived" our fortunes. This is what we need now! Please "revive" us, showing "mercy" and giving "saving help."

In the psalm we then ponder on who God is. In the next three stanzas we focus on attributes of God that we must take into account. God is merciful but he is also just. In the first stanza we learn that, if we turn to God in our "hearts," his gift to us is "peace." If we stand in awe of him ("fear him"), he will help us. We will see his "glory" abiding with us, in our very midst. In the second stanza we hear of the fusion of qualities. "Mercy and faithfulness have met." Human "faithfulness" has attracted God's "mercy." We have been forgiven! "Justice and peace have embraced." These two attributes of God have joined together, both being given to human beings. We will become faithful; God will pour justice on us from heaven. In the third stanza we are told that because of our faithfulness God will give us "prosperity," abiding with us in justice and peace.

If we read the psalm from a Christian point of view, we can rejoice over what the incarnation of Jesus brought about for us. Truly, when Jesus came, God forgave us all our "guilt" and covered our "sins." He favored his "land," the whole world in which now every soul is redeemed. Jesus came bringing "mercy" and "saving help." The message of Jesus is ever "peace" for those who turn to him in their "hearts." Jesus has promised to be with us always, ever giving us his "saving help."

What happened with the coming of Jesus? "Mercy and faithfulness have met; justice and peace have embraced." All these qualities have been found in Jesus. He was faithful even unto death, pouring his mercy upon us. He paid the price of sin, as justice required, and, by so doing, gave us the gift of his peace. If we are faithful to Jesus, our souls will live in the richness of his gaze attended by "justice" and "peace." The quotation from Origen at the start of the psalm well presents these lessons: "God blessed the land when our Savior came to earth."

Canticle: Isaiah 26:1-4, 7-9, 12

In these lines we speak to God directly in our own voice and in that of the Church. As in Psalm 85, we hear of features of human beings that attract God's favor. This canticle is a song of triumph. We have "accomplished" great things. It is through God's help that we have "a strong city." Our part has been to strive to be "just" and keep "faith."

We say to God: "You keep in peace" those who have "firm purpose" and who "trust in you." We are urged to "trust" God forever because he is "an eternal Rock." God himself is just and he helps those who are just. We human beings desire in our souls the qualities we find in God. Through the "night" we "yearn" for God; we keep "vigil" for him. If God is near to us, we all learn "justice." God then lavishes his peace upon us.

If we read this canticle from a Carmelite perspective, we can gaze inwardly at the "strong city," the center of our souls where God dwells. This center is our haven, a secure place in which we can abide in prayer. To enter we must be faithful and just. If our "firm purpose" is to be with God in prayer, he will bestow his peace upon us. He is worthy of all our trust. Yes, he is truly a "Rock" within.

Our efforts to be "just" will help us come into God's presence. Truly his "name" and "title" are "the desire of our souls." Inwardly, we yearn for God, especially "in the night." Then, in particular, we keep "vigil," longing for God's presence to infuse our whole being.

Psalm 67

See discussion at *Week II, Wednesday, Evening Prayer*, p. 113.

Reading: 1 John 4:14-15

In the reading we learn the crucial truth: "The Father has sent the Son as savior of the world." Something vital happens when we accept this truth that Jesus is the "Son of God": we come to dwell "in God" and he in us. Our belief opens up our soul to a divine guest. We can abide in his presence.

What is the evidence of this indwelling of God? It is indicated in the two previous verses to this reading (1 John 4:12-13). We love one another. The love which we show is God at work in our souls. We come to learn how to love more and more perfectly. "His love is brought to perfection in us." Where does the love come from? We share in the very Spirit of God, the Holy Spirit. We sense the presence of this Spirit of love within. When we show forth love to others, we can feel great joy. By loving, "we know we remain in him and he in us."

Wednesday

Psalm 86

We begin our day in direct address to God, as we pray in our own voice and in that of the Church. How do I see myself? I am "poor and needy," especially needing God's mercy. I am "faithful" and one who "trusts" in God. To God "I cry" and "lift up my soul" during the whole day. From God I hope for "mercy" and "joy." I count on God because of who he is: "good and forgiving"; "full of love." If ever I should be in trouble, I will call upon God. Surely he "will reply."

We then hear more about God. His greatness is such that all "nations" will come to "adore" him and to "glorify" his name. God is one alone and from him come all "marvellous" deeds.

I ask God: "Show me . . . your way so that I may walk in your truth." It is the heart that finds the God of love. I ask God to guide my heart that I may stand in awe of him. As I think of the present and future, longing to be close to God and to honor him, I also recall the past. My heart thrills with thanksgiving and I remember his past mercies and love. Even now I see dangers around me, but I turn in haste to God. I think of further characteristics: "mercy and compassion." God is "slow to anger" and "abounding in love and truth." From God I request "strength" and salvation. Most of all, I want him to "console me" and give me "help."

From a Christian point of view we can hear the voice of Jesus in this psalm, especially during the time of his passion. Jesus was "poor and needy." He describes himself as "meek and humble of heart" (Matthew 11:29). Paul mentions "the gentleness and clemency of Christ" (2 Corinthians 10:1). We can hear Jesus pray to his Father as his "servant," as one who lifts up his soul to him. We know that Jesus walked in the "way" of the Father, the way of "truth." Jesus affirms that God will help him in trouble, this God whom all nations will adore, who alone is God.

We can hear Jesus rejoice because the Father saved him "from the depths of the grave." He had to face the "proud" and "ruthless" during his passion and death, but the Father showed a splendid "sign of . . . favor": Jesus rose from the dead. Words resound through this psalm: "love," "truth," "mercy," "compassion." All these Jesus taught. To him beyond all others the Father turned his "ear" and gave "answer."

Canticle: Isaiah 33:13-16

In these lines God speaks to us, asking us to recognize his deeds and to "acknowledge" his power. A challenge is posed to human beings. Who among us "can live with the consuming fire" and "with the everlasting flames"? These descriptions suggest aspects of the presence of God just as we hear in Hebrews 12:29: "Our God is a consuming fire." We then find a description of those who will be able to meet this challenge. What is needed? The practice of virtue, honest speech, rejection of unlawful gain and bribes, refusal to hear of violence or to look on evil. Those who fulfill these requirements will find blessings: a lofty, safe dwelling and abundance of supplies.

Psalm 98

This beautiful psalm of praise we can sing in our own voice and that of the Church. It takes on a rich meaning if said from a Christian point of view. We can joyfully celebrate the resurrection of Jesus. We are to sing a "new song," yes, "new" because all history has been changed by what God has done. He has "worked wonders." By raising Jesus from the dead he has "brought salvation." What God has done is just: the price of sin has been paid. God has shown "his truth and love" to us who are the new "house of Israel."

This salvation is not something limited but extends to "the ends of the earth." Truly we should "ring out" our joy. The more we ponder on what God has done for the human race, the more we want to make music. Let us use "harp," "trumpets," and "sound of the horn." We want also the "sea," the "rivers," and "the world and all its peoples" to exult with gladness. Jesus has come and will come again. We can, therefore, "rejoice at the presence of the Lord." He now rules the earth and "will rule the world with justice and the peoples with fairness." This is our "new song to the Lord," a song of Easter triumph and lasting joy.

Reading: Job 1:21; 2:10b

This passage tells us starkly what we are as human beings. Job says that we were born with nothing and we die taking nothing. All comes from the Lord whose right it is to give and to remove. It is easy to accept blessings from God. It is not easy to endure distress and suffering. Job teaches us that our role is to trust and to bless God no matter what befalls us. We must cling to him in faith.

Thursday

Psalm 87

We pray this psalm in our own voice and that of the Church. From a Christian point of view we are filled with joy as we think of the Church, the new Jerusalem, the new "Zion." God loves Jerusalem, the city founded on his "holy mountain." He now lives and cherishes the new Jerusalem, the Church. Just as "Zion" was called to be "mother" to all nations, so the Church spreads the message of redemption in Christ to every person. Each of us has a place in God's holy city. We are truly God's "children." As we dance with joy, our song to everyone is that we all have a "home" in the new Jerusalem, the Church.

From a Carmelite perspective we can see in this psalm a description of God's dwelling at the center of our souls. In truth we are the new Jerusalem, each of us being a temple of the Holy Spirit. We are each a "city of God" where God himself dwells. We find our true "home" in God, whose kingdom is within. What is true of each of us is true of all who accept Christ as Savior. We can dance for joy at this knowledge and proclaim it eagerly to all peoples.

Canticle: Isaiah 40:10-17

In this canticle we find a wondrous picture of God as redeemer. In the first stanza we learn that God is ruler of the universe and he is filled with strength. In the next stanza we hear of God as "shepherd," gently caring for "lambs" and "ewes." Thus he cares for us.

We then encounter a series of questions that tell us vividly who God is. It is God who created "the waters of the sea" and "the heavens," who structured the "earth," "mountains," and "hills." These parts of creation came from the mind of God that planned all things. The next stanza, with further questions, tells us of the supremacy of God's "spirit," "knowledge," "judgment," and "understanding." No human being can grasp these aspects of God or ever comprehend his ways.

We then are given God's perspective of the universe. Nations are "as a drop of the bucket" and "as dust on the scales." The "coastlands weigh no more than powder." Nations in fact are as "nothing and void" to God. How little and insignificant we are! As we read this canticle, we associate it with Jesus. At John 10:11 we hear Jesus say: "I am the good shepherd. A good shepherd lays down his life for the sheep." How fittingly we apply to him stanza 2:

Like a shepherd he feeds his flock;
in his arms he gathers the lambs,
carrying them in his bosom,
and leading the ewes with care.

Paul twice quotes this canticle. At Romans 11:33-34 he exclaims: "Oh, the depth of the riches and wisdom and knowledge of God!" He then quotes the stanza of this canticle that refers to the wondrous mind of God. At 1 Corinthians 2:16, in speaking of those who understand spiritual matters, he again asks: "For 'who has known the mind of the Lord, so as to counsel him?'" He says that we Christians can have spiritual insight: "But we have the mind of Christ."

From a Christian point of view, therefore, the canticle tells us of Jesus as a gentle and loving shepherd. It may suggest also to us Jesus as "the image of the invisible God, the firstborn of all creation. For in him were created all things in heaven and on earth" (Colossians 1:15-16). Jesus is Lord of the universe. To him, as God, all nations may be as "nothing and void," and yet he loves each person as a gentle shepherd, his flock. We see the grandeur and glory of Christ; we stand in awe of his redeeming love.

Psalm 99

In our voice and the voice of the Church we cry out: "The Lord is king." This God is "throned on the cherubim." He rules all peoples. "He is holy, full of power." We then directly address God: "You are a king who loves what is right." In speaking to God we emphasize espe-

cially his relation to "equity, justice and right." We turn
to others and urge them to "exalt the Lord our God." We
repeat this invitation again at the end of the psalm.

We then recall what God has done in the past. We
speak of Aaron and Moses, his priests, and Samuel.
These individuals did God's "will" and kept his "law." To
them "he spoke in the pillar of cloud." Once again we
speak directly to God: "O Lord our God, you answered
them." We tell God: "For them you were a God who forgives; yet you punished all their offenses." As we see how
God treated these people, we know that he will be such
for us as well. Yes, he will punish our sins, but he will
also forgive us for them. In the psalm as a whole we see
that God is just. He establishes justice in the universe.
He is just toward human beings in that he punishes all
offenses. But, joy above joy, God is merciful and forgives.
Truly, he is holy, and we should "bow down before Zion,
his footstool," and "before his holy mountain."

Reading: 1 Peter 4:10-11a

God pours grace into human beings, grace that
allows us to serve one another. There may be the grace
of speech that will allow me to proclaim the gospel.
There may be the grace of strength that will allow one to
serve. In all instances the Source of the grace receives
glory, always, ever "through Jesus Christ."

Friday

Psalm 51

See discussion at *Week I, Friday, Morning Prayer*,
p. 41.

Canticle: Jeremiah 14:17-21

In this lament we cry out in our own voice and that of
the Church as we see destruction and pain around us.
From a Christian point of view we may weep for the

Church in her sufferings in different parts of the world. Everywhere that we visit or cast our eyes tells us of sorrow, whether in "field" or in "city." We cry out in anguish to God. We seem to be mortally wounded. We strive to wait for peace to come but, instead, we find ourselves filled with "terror." All this disaster brings self-awareness. We recognize our sinfulness and beseech God for mercy. We recall the "covenant" God made with his people and "the throne of *his* glory," the temple in Jerusalem. We plead for God's blessing on us, the new Jerusalem. We believe in the new covenant made in Jesus' blood and trust in God's faithfulness to his Church.

Taken from a Carmelite perspective, this canticle directs our attention to what may happen within our souls. The spiritual journey is one beset with difficulties and hardships. Jesus warned us that it would be so (Matthew 7:13-14): "Enter through the narrow gate; for the gate is wide and the road broad that leads to destruction, and those who enter through it are many. How narrow the gate and constricted the road that leads to life. And those who find it are few."

At times on our journey there will be darkness and aridity. As we look within our souls, we may behold only our faults and failings, our shortcomings and sins. We find no peace pervading our souls, only fear and terror. We feel overwhelmed with guilt. At such times we must hold firm to our faith. God is at the center of our souls, but the journey to him is a challenging one. We can be sure that he will be faithful. We can be confident that he will always cherish the temple of our soul.

Psalm 100

Ah, what a different message and tone this joyous psalm has from that of the canticle! Our souls have experienced refreshment. God has smiled again on us as individuals and as members of his Church. We have felt his blessings once again. We, therefore, summon others: "Cry out with joy to the Lord, all the earth." We are to "serve the Lord with gladness." We are to "come before him, singing for joy."

Who are we? The people of God, the flock of God. No, more still! He "made us" and "we belong to him." What a relationship to cherish! We are creatures of God's own making and his cherished belongings. Our response is to be one of endless thanksgiving, as we sing "songs of praise" and "bless" God. What is God like? He is "good." His love is "merciful" and "eternal." He is ever "faithful."

Reading: 2 Corinthians 12:9b-10

Paul tells us the secret of Christian activity. We do not act, but Jesus acts in us. If we claim any strength coming from human nature and count on it, Jesus cannot act in us. We make him weak. Paul says that he boasts of his weakness in order that "the power of Christ" may rest upon him. He says that he is "content" with all sorts of things that call for strength: "weakness, . . . mistreatment, . . . distress, . . . persecutions and difficulties." These he sees as opportunities to draw on the strength of Jesus. The more powerless he is in himself, the stronger Jesus can be in him.

Saturday

Psalm 119:145-152

See discussion at *Week I, Saturday, Morning Prayer,* p. 45.

Canticle: Wisdom 9:1-6, 9-11

In 1 Kings 3:6-9 and 2 Chronicles 1:8-10 Solomon prays for "Wisdom." In this canticle we have another version of this prayer. We can pray this canticle in our voice and in the voice of the Church, crying out, like Solomon, for the wondrous gift of "Wisdom." From a

Christian point of view, we relate this request for "Wisdom" to Jesus "in whom are hidden all the treasures of wisdom and knowledge" (Colossians 2:3). Twice Paul tells us of Jesus:

"We proclaim Christ crucified . . . Christ the power of God and the wisdom of God" (1 Corinthians 1:23-24).

"It is due to [God] that you are in Christ Jesus, who became for us wisdom from God, as well as righteousness, sanctification, and redemption" (1 Corinthians 1:30).

We wish to share in something that Jesus fully exemplifies and we ask to receive "Wisdom."

We address this prayer, speaking directly to God. God is "Lord of mercy." God created the whole universe ("all things") by his "word." Once again, from the Christian point of view, we think of Jesus, the Word, of whom John tells us: "All things came to be through him, / and without him nothing came to be" (1:3). We learn that human beings were given a special role in the universe: to "rule" creatures, to "govern . . . in holiness and justice," and to "render judgment in integrity of heart."

We ask God for "Wisdom." We recognize that we cannot easily fulfill the mission given to us human beings by God. Why? We are "weak," "short-lived," and "lacking in comprehension of judgment and of laws." We realize that all other blessings from God do not make for success if "Wisdom" is lacking.

Who is "Wisdom"? A presence with God, abiding with God always, and especially when God created the universe. Once again we recall what John says of Jesus as the Word: "In the beginning was the Word, / and the Word was with God, / and the Word was God. / He was in the beginning with God" (1:1-2). Wisdom, the canticle tells us, "understands" what pleases God and what is "conformable" to his will. We long to be filled with "Wisdom" so that our actions may be in accord with God's will and be pleasing to him. We hear more about "Wisdom": "She knows and understands all things." Once again the reference to "all things" refers to the whole universe. There is nothing that escapes the knowledge and understanding of "wisdom."

What effect do we hope to have if "Wisdom" becomes our gift? She will "guide" us "discreetly" in our affairs and "safeguard" us as by her own "glory." From the Christian point of view, we long for Jesus to be with us, guiding us by his Holy Spirit and protecting us with the glory that he had "before the world began" (John 17:5). Jesus has promised to be with us always: "And behold, I am with you always, until the end of the age" (Matthew 28:20). In this canticle we ask for him to be present, especially as "wise" redeemer and guide.

Psalm 117

See discussion at *Week I, Saturday, Morning Prayer*, p. 47.

Reading: Philippians 2:14-15

In this passage Paul gives us advice on how to act with wisdom. In our actions we are not to grumble nor to argue. Instead, we are to manifest a simple obedience, showing ourselves "innocent and straightforward." Our calling is to reveal to the world that we are "children of God." What a privileged title we bear! We are to shine among others like "stars in the sky." In this context we may recall Daniel 12:3:

But the wise shall shine brightly
　like the splendor of the firmament,
And those who lead the many to justice
　shall be like the stars forever.

We have prayed for Wisdom in the canticle. Infused with it, we will reflect forth its glory to those whom we meet.

II: Evening Prayer

Sunday, Evening Prayer I

Psalm 113

In this psalm which we can pray in our voice and that of the Church, we hear a call to praise God. His "name" deserves to be praised through all time ("evermore") and through the whole world ("from the rising of the sun to its setting"). Why does he deserve such praise? His glory extends far beyond the nations and the universe. Even though he is so lofty, this God cares for us. He "stoops . . . to look down upon heaven and earth." He need not do so but he does! We then hear on which people God directs his gaze. Not on the rich, the powerful, the mighty. No, "he lifts up the lowly"; "he raises the poor." He puts these in lofty places. He remembers the "childless wife" and blesses her "with children."

The last stanza reminds us of the canticle of Mary (see chapter 5, pp. 192-197). Mary also speaks of God noticing her as a "lowly servant." God lifts up "the lowly," doing "great things" for us. We recall that Mary sang her canticle to Elizabeth, a "childless wife" who was blessed miraculously in her old age with a son, John the Baptist. We likewise are glad because we can look for God's mercy and compassion to us in our lowly state.

Psalm 116:10-19

(For Psalm 116:1-9 see discussion at *Week II, Friday, Evening Prayer*, p. 118.)

This psalm of trust and thanksgiving we can pray in our own voice and in that of the Church. We begin in the first person, declaring our confidence in God. "I trusted even when I said: 'I am sorely afflicted.' " At this time I turned to human beings for help and found no one to support me.

The next two stanzas take on a rich meaning if we alter them to direct address:

How can I repay *you*, Lord,
for *your* goodness to me?
The cup of salvation I will raise:
I will call on *your name, O Lord.*

My vows to *you*, Lord, I will fulfill
before all *your* people.
O precious in *your eyes, O Lord,*
is the death of *your* faithful.

God has been good to me. My response will be to raise the "cup of salvation." Before other people "I will fulfill" vows I have made to God. From a Christian point of view we can see here a desire to take part in the Eucharist, to share in the rite that proclaims our salvation. We will do so by joining others, relating to them the great blessing we have received.

In the next stanza I address God directly, telling him that I am his "servant." I conclude the psalm by once again declaring my intention to make a "thanksgiving sacrifice" and to "fulfill" my vows. In the light of the great blessings that God has bestowed on me, I wish to tell many of how my trust in him was well placed.

In this psalm we can hear also the voice of Jesus after his resurrection. Before his crucifixion he was "sorely afflicted." There was no one in whom he could trust. But the Father raised him from the dead. Now he can be filled with endless thanksgiving. God has "loosened" his bonds. In so doing, the Father has also made Jesus the cause for our thanksgiving. We too can trust God endlessly.

Canticle: Philippians 2:6-11

See discussion at *Week I, Sunday, Evening Prayer I,* p. 51.

Reading: Hebrews 13:20-21

In this blessing from the end of Hebrews we hear of the action of the Father in raising Jesus from the dead. The death of Jesus on the cross established a new "covenant." The blessing asks that the Father, "the God of peace" give us "all that is good." The effect of this goodness will be that we will carry out his "will." He will do so in us "through Jesus Christ." Jesus will live in our hearts and, by his presence and his grace, will enable us to do the Father's will. Yes, truly, we cry out: "To Christ be glory forever!"

Sunday, Evening Prayer II

Psalm 110:1-5, 7

See discussion at *Week I, Sunday, Evening Prayer II,* p. 52.

Psalm 111

This psalm, spoken in the first person, we can utter in our own voice and that of the Church. It becomes especially meaningful if expressed in direct address.

> I will thank *you*, Lord, with all my heart
> in the meeting of the just and their assembly.
> Great are *your works, O Lord;*
> to be pondered by all who love them.

I say that I will praise God in the presence of others. What delights me most are God's works, worthy to be "pondered." We are called on to discern God's works, to "love" them and to strive to understand them.

> Majestic and glorious *your* work,
> *your* justice stands firm for ever.
> *You make* us remember *your* wonders.
> *You, Lord,* are compassion and love.

In these lines we sum up what God does. His works, "majestic and glorious," are "justice," "compassion" and "love." As we discern these aspects of what God does, we are filled with awe.

You give food to those who fear *you;*
keep your covenant ever in mind.
You have shown *your* might to *your* people
by giving them the lands of the nations.

We hear of specific actions of God. He feeds us. He has a permanent relationship with us. He has shown himself strong in our defense. From the Christian point of view we think gratefully of the food of the Eucharist. We bless God for the new "covenant" he has established with us through the passion, death, and resurrection of Jesus. We rejoice that the Christian message is for the whole world.

Your works are justice and truth:
your precepts are all of them sure,
standing firm for ever and ever:
they are made in uprightness and truth.

In these lines we see the essence of God's works: "justice and truth." With these foundations we can be boundlessly confident in what God does. All that he commands for human beings, his "precepts," rest on these same foundations. They will last always.

You have sent deliverance to your people
and established *your* covenant for ever.
Holy is *your* name, to be feared.

To fear *you, Lord,* is the first stage of wisdom;
all who do so prove themselves wise.
Your praise shall last for ever.

Once again we hear of God's eternal covenant. We learn more of God: he is holy. We "fear" God, that is, we stand in awe of his holiness. This attitude is the very basis of being wise: it is "the first stage of wisdom."

What we will always discover is that God deserves end-less praise.

Canticle: Revelation 19:1-7

See discussion at *Week I, Sunday, Evening Prayer II,* p. 55.

Reading: 1 Peter 1:3-5

In these lines we hear of the wondrous action of God the Father. In "mercy" he gave new lives to all of us: we have "new birth." What is the essence of this "new birth"? "Hope" that is based on one event: the resurrection of Jesus from the dead. What kind of birth is it? "To an imperishable inheritance, incapable of fading or defilement." Where is it? In heaven.

Peter then says that all of us who have been reborn into this hope have a great treasure: faith. It is by our faith that God protects us. The "birth" we await is one to "salvation" that will be "revealed" at the end of time. All of us have been born anew, vibrant with a life drawn from the risen Jesus and buoyed up with hope of eternal salvation. With joy we praise the merciful Father who has given us all these gifts.

Monday

Psalm 123

In the first and third stanzas of this psalm we address God directly, appealing in our own voice and that of the Church for mercy. My position is a lowly one: I look up with hope to God who dwells in the heavens. I am like a "slave" or a "servant," looking incessantly for "mercy." We then pray for ourselves and for others, asking once again for "mercy." We have suffered at the hands of the proud but God's compassion is our hope.

Psalm 124

In this brief psalm we pray with thanksgiving that God came to our rescue in trouble. Only because the Lord was "on our side" did we survive. On a physical level our enemies were stronger than we. In the next stanza we have a reference perhaps to the parting of the Red Sea. We had nowhere to go except into the waters and there only death awaited. We would have been swept away! But it was not to be so. Instead, we escaped like a bird from a snare. We "flew" free. Who was our helper? The One who created "heaven and earth."

Canticle: Ephesians 1:3-10

See discussion at *Week I, Monday, Evening Prayer,* p. 58.

Reading: James 4:11-12

In this passage we are exhorted not to "speak ill of one another." Jesus has told us: we are not "to judge" (Matthew 7:1-5). If we do, we break the "law" to love our neighbor as ourselves. We are not to adopt a superior stance to anyone. Such a position belongs only to God who is "Lawgiver and Judge." Our call is simply to love.

Tuesday

Psalm 125

In this psalm we encounter several striking images. First about ourselves. When we trust God, we become like an unshakable mountain, standing firm and secure. We are like the mountains that surround Jerusalem. Second about God. He too is like the mountains surrounding Jerusalem, strong, magnificent, holding us in his embrace. We need not fear that the wicked will ever get complete control. God will not allow this. We pray that God will bless us who strive to be "good" and "upright of heart." Our greatest wish is for "peace."

Psalm 131

In this lovely psalm we speak directly to God in our own voice. We hear too the voice of the Church, the Church as it is meant to be, the lowly, humble servant of God. I tell God: "My heart is not proud nor haughty my eyes." This is my condition. I do not claim as my own what is a gift. I do not strut proudly about, looking with contempt on others. All my longing, all my wishes are for the simple and true. I have not sought "things . . . beyond me."

What have I done? "I have set my soul in silence and peace." My soul is like a child sleeping in its "mother's arms." Deep peace pervades my being as I rest humbly in God's presence.

As we pray the psalm, one image that may enter our minds is that of the Madonna and child. We see Mary gently holding Jesus, cherishing this precious child. We imagine the calm and peace that this baby experiences in these faithful and loving arms So we can envision our soul within us. We can imagine also that God holds us in this way, so sweetly, so safely. We eagerly place our "hope in the Lord both now and for ever."

Canticle: Revelation: 4:11; 5:9, 10, 12

See discussion at *Week I, Tuesday, Evening Prayer,* p. 61.

Reading: Romans 12:9-12

This passage presents us with several exhortations. First, we are to love one another and in a sincere way. Our love is to be as strong as that for family members. One feature of this love will be the deep "respect" we accord each other.

In our choices we are to "detest what is evil" and to "cling to what is good." In so doing, we are to be zeal-

ous: "fervent in spirit." Our service goes to God—this
we must remember. When things look bright and
promising, we are to "rejoice in hope." If we are in distress, we are to be "patient under trial." Always, in all
circumstances, we are called to "persevere in prayer."
The ground of all our behavior is "love." It shows us
how to relate to one another. It feeds our enthusiastic
service. It teaches us how to behave in all circumstances, both positive and negative. Prayer that is constant will bring us into the presence of God, the source
of all our love.

Wednesday

Psalm 126

In this song full of hope and joy, we speak in our own
voice and in that of the Church. We begin by remembering God's merciful intervention in the past. He delivered
us "from bondage." Here we probably have a reference
to the escape of the Israelites through the Red Sea.
Truly this event was like a marvelous dream! How we
laughed with joy as we recalled the miraculous way in
which we were freed. What songs we sang! Others saw
how blessed we had been. Our gladness knew no
bounds. Now we see ourselves in bondage once again,
but God is our hope. We may feel like a "dry land." To
us God will be like "streams." We may sow "in tears,"
but we will "reap" with singing. The last stanza repeats
this image: tears accompany sowing; songs, reaping.

This psalm gives us a message of hope. If we are in
difficult circumstances, we can count on God for deliverance. With his "streams" he may save us from situations which we have watered with our "tears." From a
Carmelite perspective, we can think of times of dryness
and aridity that may bring us intense suffering within.

We believe that God is at the center of our souls, but all seems to be dry. Nonetheless we must persevere in prayer, constantly "sowing" seeds of love and concern for others. God will make his presence felt again in the soul. Then there will be "laughter." Then there will be songs!

Psalm 127

In this psalm we build on the ideas in the previous one. All fruitful activity comes from the Lord. The psalmist tells us clearly: the Lord is to "build"; the Lord is to "watch." If we do not act under the influence of grace, striving to do God's will, our actions are "in vain." All our efforts for our own projects, rising early and working late, will come to nothing if God is not with us. When God pleases, he pours gifts on his "beloved" even while they are asleep. One such gift for human beings comes in the form of strong sons able to defend their fathers.

As Christians we can read this psalm in the light of the grace won for us by Jesus. He truly was "a gift from the Lord, a blessing." He was a source of joy to his Father. With the help of his grace we can "build" and "watch" for eternity.

Canticle: Colossians 1:12-20

See discussion at *Week I, Wednesday, Evening Prayer,* p. 64.

Reading: Ephesians 3:20-21

We pick up again the theme of God's grace at work in us. Paul tells us that God's "power" works wonders. It "can do immeasurably more than we ask or imagine." We recognize that this power can operate in our very souls. Paul speaks a beautiful prayer that for all time "glory" be to the Father both "in the church and in Christ Jesus," the founder and cornerstone of this

Church. Always we are to praise God for his marvelous
works.

Thursday

Psalm 132–I

This psalm recalls the events narrated in 2 Samuel 7
when David was determined to build a temple for God
but was told that his son would fulfill this task. In part
I of this psalm we ask God to recall how zealous David
was about founding "a dwelling for the Strong One of
Jacob." We hear of how he and others found the ark,
containing the precious "law." This ark was God's
"dwelling" and his "footstool." We pray that God will
now abide in the "place of *his* rest" in his temple in
Jerusalem. We make this request in the name of David
who was faithful. We know that, if God is with us,
"priests" will be holy and the "faithful" full of joy.

Psalm 132–II

In 2 Samuel 7 we learn that God swore to make the
line of David firm and lasting. Part II of Psalm 132 mentions this oath. We hear what God promises to David's
descendants if they are faithful in observing his
"covenant in truth" and in keeping his "laws." They too
will continue to rule during the ages to come.

Why does God make these promises? He loves Zion
and has chosen it "for his dwelling." He affirms: "This
is my resting-place for ever." God directly addresses us,
telling us how he will bless Zion. She will produce
much. Her "poor" will have bread. Her priests will find
"salvation"; her faithful will sing for "joy." Light will
shine for David's line while his enemies are defeated.

If we read this whole psalm from a Christian point of
view, it takes on a rich meaning for us. When Gabriel
speaks to Mary, he tells her of Jesus (Luke 1:32): "He

will be great and will be called Son of the Most High, and the Lord God will give him the throne of David his father, and he will rule over the house of Jacob forever, and of his kingdom there will be no end."

Jesus has inherited the throne of David. He truly founded a "dwelling" for the Lord, the Church. Throughout the world this Church (and every individual church) becomes a "place of rest" for God. In this Church, filled with God's presence, priests are "clothed with holiness" and the faithful are full of "joy." As we hear of the ark where the precious scrolls of the Torah are stored, we recall with reverence and gratitude that Jesus abides, as a living presence, in the Blessed Sacrament in our tabernacles. Before him we humbly kneel, acknowledging his Real Presence among us.

In Part II we can hear of God's love for the new "Zion," the Church. We rejoice to hear that the Church is his "resting-place" and that he chooses "to live" in her. Since God is with his Church, he pours abundant blessings upon her. She becomes a source of blessings for others as she bears abundant fruit. Again we hear of the "holiness" of her priests and the "joy" of her faithful. Jesus is the "anointed" one of God, the "Christ." God "will prepare a lamp" for his anointed; "on him" God's "crown shall shine." Jesus is the "light of the world" (John 8:12). In Revelation 21:23 he, as Lamb of God, is the "light" of the new city of God. Jesus overcame all "enemies" in his resurrection, especially the enemies of sin and death. On Jesus God's "crown shall shine" since he is forever "Lord of lords and king of kings" (Revelation 17:14).

Canticle: Revelation 11:17-18; 12:10b-12a

See discussion at *Week I, Thursday, Evening Prayer,* p. 69.

Reading: 1 Peter 3:8-9

In this passage we find a description of what our Christian behavior should ideally be. We are to strive to be "like-minded" with others. We are to be "sympathetic" and "kindly disposed" to them. Our position is to be "humble." Overall we are to love others. Life may pose challenges. People will inflict evil on us or insult us. We, however, must try to live the teaching of Jesus. Under these circumstances we will, therefore, "return a blessing." Our actions will not be in vain because these blessings, given to others, become our very own "inheritance."

Friday

Psalm 135–I

We sing this psalm in our voice and that of the Church as we summon others to praise God. The psalm speaks of the deliverance of Israel from bondage in Egypt. From a Christian point of view we rejoice at our redemption from sin and death through the merciful action of God in sending us Jesus. In the first stanza we call on those in the "house of the Lord" to praise him. The second stanza tells us why God deserves praise. He is "good." He is "loving." He has chosen us to be his special "possession."

Stanzas three and four tell us more about God. He is "great." He does his will through all creation, "in heaven, on earth, in the seas." All natural phenomena occur at his bidding: clouds, lightning, rain, wind. He is Lord of the universe.

We hear of the way in which God rescued Israel. We, the new Israel, have been saved in even more wonderful ways. God has given us salvation as a free gift by the death of his own Son. He has invited all peoples to belong to this Church, saving us all from the bondage of sin.

Psalm 135–II

The second part of this psalm carries on the theme of praise. We learn more about who God is. First, we hear about the "name" of God. Speaking in direct address, we affirm that this "name" is one that "stands for ever." From age to age we call upon God. His "name," indicating his very essence and being, extends ever through time. Second, we focus on two attributes of God: he is "just" and he shows "pity."

In the next two stanzas we find descriptions of idols. They are lifeless with no power or capabilities. These descriptions warn us in our time not to make idols for ourselves. It is very easy to do. We can begin to believe that wealth, position, status, or security are what bring us power and safety. Such things may not be just; they may not include pity for others; they certainly do not stand forever. But in God are all of these traits, and it is in him that we must place our confidence and trust.

The final stanzas give our response: the rejection of idols. Worship of idols makes us "like them": powerless and lifeless. Worship of God fills us with his grace and makes us receivers of his "justice" and "pity." Thus we can summon all people to "bless the Lord." God dwells in the new Jerusalem, the Church. From there he sheds his love on all peoples.

Canticle: Revelation 15:3-4

See discussion at *Week I, Friday, Evening Prayer*, p. 72.

Reading: James 1:2-4

In this passage we encounter the paradox of Christianity. On a natural level we grieve when trials come. On a Christian level we rejoice. Christianity turns responses upside down and sets us on a path of "pure joy." Trials test our faith. It becomes stronger and we find in our souls a new "endurance." The more "endurance" we nurture, the more we will be "mature." In maturity, James suggests, we lack nothing. We grow more and more like Jesus, our model of endurance and trust.

4.

Week IV: Morning and Evening Prayer

*In the rich depths of silence we hear
your summons to love.*

I: Morning Prayer

Sunday

Psalm 118

See discussion at *Week II, Sunday, Morning Prayer,*
p. 75.

Canticle: Daniel 3:52-57

See discussion at *Week II, Sunday, Morning Prayer,*
p. 77.

Psalm 150

See discussion at *Week II, Sunday, Morning Prayer,*
p. 78.

Reading: 2 Timothy 2:8,11-13

This reading proclaims the essential truth of
Christianity: Jesus is risen from the dead. Our faith
rests on this truth. We then encounter verses that may
have come from a Christian hymn. These lines suggest
our relationship with Jesus. First, we are to die "with
him," both in baptism and in the sufferings of our
Christian journey. If we do, our hope is sure: "We shall
also live with him." If in our lives we "hold out to the
end," our hope is richer still, to "reign" with Jesus.

If, in contrast, by acts of free will, we "deny" Jesus,
he will honor our free will. He will not force himself
upon us. We may be "unfaithful" but Jesus will never be
such. If we are faithless and turn from him, we can still

be sure that if we return, we will find him "faithful," even loving and merciful. Jesus will always be true to his own nature: he is our savior and redeemer. In him our hopes can be firmly placed.

Monday

Psalm 90

In our own voice and that of the Church we say this psalm in direct address to God. We tell God: "You have been our refuge from one generation to the next." We focus on one feature of God: his existence is forever, predating the universe. "You are God, without beginning or end." His view of time is very different from ours. "A thousand years are like yesterday, come and gone, no more than a watch in the night."

In relation to human beings God's power is absolute. Our lives are swiftly over and we return "to dust." Our lives are like the "grass," springing up quickly and soon fading away. From God we can hide nothing. He knows all our guilt and our secrets. How short is our span of days: "Our life is over like a sigh." We recall how much "emptiness and pain" fill our years.

In our human lives we can never understand God, who is far beyond our comprehension. We thus utter our prayer:

Make us know the shortness of life
that we may gain wisdom of heart.

To God we say: "In the morning, fill us with your love." We ask for "joy" to replace all our "affliction." We wish to experience God's "work" and "glory." It is God who will give "success to the work of our hands."

From a Carmelite perspective we ponder on who God is as he dwells in the center of our hearts. We say: Yes, God, you are our "refuge." Always "you are . . . without beginning or end." Our wonder is great: it is you, God, who inhabit the core of our beings. Yes, our life is fragile, quickly over. We view time so differently from you, God. You control our lives completely, and we can hide nothing from you. Why? Because you are in our very souls, aware of our "guilt" and our "secrets."

Who of us understands you? What we need to know is the "shortness of our life." You within are eternal and can fill us with love. Yes, let us begin our day in this way, full of your love and joy "in the morning." Let your "glory" come from within and suffuse our beings. From your power and favor our success will come.

Canticle: Isaiah 42:10-16

In this canticle we hear the voice of God who promises to come into his world and to work wondrous changes. We begin with an invitation to "sing to the Lord" in a new way. We are to utter a song that will fill the whole world, "from the top of the mountains" and "in the coastlands." Why are we to sing? Because God is manifesting his power and strength to us, coming among his people.

What is God like? "A hero, . . . a warrior." He overcomes those who oppose him. Then the canticle has God speak in the first-person. God tells us: In earlier times I endured in silence what I saw on earth but now I will cry out in anguish for the pain of my people. I will act. Where I must, I will bring destruction. But, most of all, I will show mercy. How? By leading the "blind" on new paths. By giving the blind sight, turning "darkness into light before them," and by making "crooked ways straight." God will come to help us to see, to show us how to live uprightly, and to transform our lives into righteousness.

Psalm 135:1-12

See discussion at *Week III, Friday, Evening Prayer*, p. 152.

Reading: Judith 8:25-27

This passage tells us to view trials and testing in the light of faith. These things have a purpose in God's plan. They do not indicate an absence of love on his part for us. On the contrary, they show that he cares for our spiritual growth and development. Thus we should be grateful for them! Figures from the past teach us that this is so: Abraham, Isaac, Jacob. There is no question here of God exacting "vengeance," but God is admonishing us to lead us to a better way of acting.

Yet these experiences are painful: the Lord places us in a "crucible" to try our hearts. But such sufferings show that we "are close to him." The result will turn out to be a blessing. For this we can give thanks.

Tuesday

Psalm 101

This psalm is spoken in the first-person. We can pray it in our own voice or in the voice of the Church. We can hear in it also the voice of Jesus, telling us what behavior of ours meets his favor and what behavior in us he will need to redeem. In the psalm we address God directly. How close he is! The second part of the introductory antiphon highlights what we desire: "I will learn from you the way of perfection."

I begin by describing my song. What are its themes? "Mercy and justice." These summarize two essential features of God: he is merciful and just. It is to God that I sing. My aim is one only: to "walk in the way of perfection." Clearly this "way" will involve "mercy and justice." But I know that I can show forth neither without God's help: "O when, Lord, will you come?"

What does walking in perfection involve? Walking "with blameless heart within my house." Not setting "before my eyes whatever is base." I will turn from evil "ways" and from those who practice evil. I will seek friends among those who likewise strive to walk in "the way of perfection." I will avoid deceitful and lying people. "Morning by morning" my aim will be to bring an end to evil deeds.

As we hear the voice of Jesus, we recognize that the themes of his life were mercy and justice. He had compassion on all sinners and died for us. He satisfied all claims of justice by taking our sins upon himself. Jesus was ever perfect, walking in "the way of perfection." Jesus has told us: "Be perfect, just as your heavenly Father is perfect" (Matthew 5:48). Certainly Jesus had a "blameless heart"; he never set before his eyes "whatever is base." He redeemed all human beings including the "crooked," the "false-hearted," the "wicked," slanderers, and all the proud and haughty. He redeemed also the deceitful and the lying. Jesus came to call all to salvation: he wants us to "dwell" with him.

Jesus now "lives forever to make intercession" for us (Hebrews 7:25). "Morning by morning," therefore, he redeems his people. By pouring grace into our hearts he makes it possible for us, like him, to walk "in the way of perfection."

From a Carmelite perspective this psalm is very rich in meaning. It is from here that Teresa of Avila derived the title of her work, *The Way of Perfection.* I address God who dwells in my heart, focusing on "mercy and justice." When these two characteristics abound in my heart, I know that I am on "the way of perfection." For the Carmelite soul this "way" leads inward, moving to an encounter with God at the core of my being. "Within my house" is within my very soul. There, in God's presence, I can walk "with blameless heart." Abiding here in deep prayer, I will reject all evil ways, especially those that I find in my own nature. Here I can see so clearly what is "base," "crooked," "false," "wicked," or "deceitful" in myself. I can recognize what is "proud" and "haughty." Absorbed in prayer, in the center of my soul, I will strive, morning by morning, to remove from my soul anything that leads to evil. Suffused by God's presence and grace, I will learn "the way of perfection."

Canticle: Daniel 3:26, 27, 29, 34-41

This canticle is the prayer of Azariah as he walked in the fiery furnace. As part of an astounding miracle in which he found coolness and safety instead of the fiery death he had freely chosen, Azariah is portrayed as speaking for his people. First, he blesses God who is "praiseworthy" and whose name is "glorious." Second, we hear why God can be described in these ways. It is because his deeds and ways are "just," "faultless," and "right." The way he has treated his people has been correct: his "judgments" are "proper."

Azariah then acknowledges that God's people have sinned. They need God's mercy, and Azariah appeals to God to remember Abraham, Isaac, and Israel. We hear about the pitiful state these people are now in. But something good has come from their sufferings. Now their hearts are "contrite" and their spirits, "humble." Their determination is to "follow" God unreservedly. Azariah knows very clearly: those who trust in God are not "put to shame." Azariah knows! He is safe in the fiery furnace! He proclaims about his people: "We follow you with our whole heart."

If we pray this canticle from a Christian perspective, we see that God has always treated human beings in the same way. Ever his deeds are "just," "faultless," and "right." We too have sinned and need God's "mercy." We, however, hope that God will ever remember Jesus and his sacrifice on Calvary. We Christians have become in number "like the stars of heaven" or "the sand on the shore of the sea." Unlike the people of Israel, we have the Church which can offer in the Eucharist the time-less sacrifice of Jesus as he redeems us from our sins. As we attend the Eucharist, we come "with contrite heart and humble spirit." In this way we ask that our "sacrifice" be accepted by God. What is our attitude to be? We are to follow God "unreservedly" and "with our whole heart." We stand in awe of God and pray to him.

Psalm 144:1-10

In this psalm we cry out in our voice and that of the Church to God. If we place parts of stanzas one and two into direct address, we come very close to God.

Blessed *are you*, Lord, my rock. . . .

You are my love, my fortress;
you are my stronghold, my savior,
my shield, my place of refuge.
You bring peoples under my rule.

Who is God for me? First, he is the object of my affec-tions. Second, he is all kind of defense for me: "strong-hold," "shield," "place of refuge." Third, he is my source of salvation: "my savior." He strengthens me for the tasks that face me.

Now I address God and ask why he loves human beings so excessively. What are we, after all? "A breath, whose life fades like a passing shadow." Yet I can call on God and his strength. He then saves me "from the mighty waters" and from all my enemies. I end my prayer by promising to sing to this God who gives us "victory."

We learn from this psalm that God deeply loves us. He is the object of our devotion: our "love." He is the source of all our security and strength. Mysterious it may be that he cares for us, but he does. He rescues us from danger. How rightly we sing to him!

Reading: Isaiah 55:1

In this passage we hear the invitation extended to us by God. We are thirsty: "Come to the water!" We are poor: "Come . . . and eat." We are invited to rich fare: "wine and milk." We know that God is inviting us to a rich life of grace in him. He will suffuse our souls with mercy and love. He invites us also to come to the Eucharist where we have the Bread of life to eat and the Wine of Christ's blood. God asks for no merits on our part: "without paying and without cost." We are to be hungry and thirsty for divine life, and he will fill us beyond measure.

Wednesday

Psalm 108

We sing this psalm in direct address to God in our own voice and that of the Church. I start off in great joy, saying to God: "My heart is ready." My heart wants to sing out its joy in praise of God. I am filled with thanksgiving to God because of two of his characteristics: his "love" and "truth." I pray for God's help.

We then hear God speak in the psalm. He says that he will establish his authority over all parts of the world. We pray to this God to help us since with him we will "do bravely."

From a Carmelite perspective, we can focus on God's actions in our souls. Trusting that God dwells within, I tell God: "My heart is ready" to give praise. Over my whole being God extends his control. His "love reaches to the heavens" and his "truth to the skies." I can understand God's words of authority over parts of the world as an affirmation of his control also of my body and soul. I am convinced that I can overcome my inner foes—all my faults, failings, and sins—with God's help. With his aid I am not afraid and I shall "do bravely."

Canticle: Isaiah 61:10—62:5

The quotation from Revelation 21:2 at the beginning of this canticle tells us the essence of this passage: "I saw the holy city, new Jerusalem, with the beauty of a bride adorned for her husband." The canticle describes in lyric joy his vision of a new Jerusalem. From the Christian point of view we see a picture of the Church rejoicing in the salvation brought by Jesus.

I speak in my own voice, saying that all my joy is in God. Why? "He has clothed me with a robe of salvation, / and wrapped me in a mantle of justice." Just as a garden brings forth luxuriant growth, the Lord, in the Church, will cause "justice and praise" to appear in all nations. All Christians are now gathered together into one new city, the new Jerusalem. She will have a "new name / pronounced by the mouth of the Lord." What is the Church? "A glorious crown in the hand of the Lord, / a royal diadem held by your God." Instead of being called "Forsaken" or "Desolate," she is "My delight" and "Espoused." The Church is the bride of Christ and she "has made herself ready" (Revelation 19:7). "For the Lord delights" in the Church and has made her "his spouse." Just "as a bridegroom rejoices in his bride, / so shall . . . God rejoice" in his Church.

From a Carmelite perspective, this canticle speaks of the beauty of every human soul. The soul has become "like a bridegroom adorned with a diadem, like a bride bedecked with her jewels." God is the "joy" of this soul. What has God done for me? "He has clothed me with a robe of salvation." In my soul God will make "justice and praise" blossom.

What will happen to my soul? I will have a new name! My soul will become "a glorious crown in the hand of the Lord, a royal diadem held by God." My soul will be for God "delight" and "espoused." God "delights" in my soul and makes it "his spouse." Jesus has told us (John

14:23): "Whoever loves me will keep my word, and my Father will love him, and we will come to him and make our dwelling with him." God will make my soul his home. He will also make it his "bride." Thus "I rejoice heartily in the Lord."

Psalm 146

In this lovely song, I speak to my soul, declaring that I will always praise God. We can sing this psalm in our own voice and that of the Church. The psalm proceeds to give advice: place no trust in human beings, even those who are strong. We are but mortals, fragile as breath. All our plans too depend on our fragile existence. What is the best source of help? God. In him alone should we place our "hope."

The remainder of the psalm gives us a list of attributes of God. He is creator of "heaven and earth, the seas and all they contain." We then hear of acts of mercy of God and those in particular who receive it: the "oppressed," the "hungry," the "imprisoned," and the "blind." His compassion reaches out to those "bowed down," the "stranger," the "widow and orphan." God loves the "just" but hinders those who do evil. This God will reign forever. What joy to know that he is full of compassion!

From a Christian point of view we see in this picture of God attributes true of Jesus. He had great compassion for the "oppressed," "hungry," "stranger," and "prisoners." He urged us to have the same, telling us that when we care for these people, we care for him (Matthew 25:35-36). How often he healed the "blind!" Those who were "bowed down" found new hope in Jesus. He knew that his mother, who was a widow, would soon lose her son. With what mercy and kindness did he restore the young man to his mother, the widow of Nain (Luke 7:11-17)! Now that Jesus is risen, we know that he will reign forever. Jesus perfectly revealed the Father to us who is described so well in this psalm. His essential nature is one of mercy.

Reading: Deuteronomy 4:39-40a

In this passage we are called on to recognize the sovereignty of God: he rules "the heavens" and the "earth." Eagerly we are to obey what he commands.

Thursday

Psalm 143:1-11

We pray this cry of distress in our own voice and that of the Church. We can hear in these lines also the voice of Jesus as he suffered in Gethsemane and on the way to Calvary. The psalm is presented in direct address as we make our appeal to God. First, I cry out to God: "Listen." I can trust that God will listen because he is "faithful" and "just." I am not asking God to judge me. I know my sins and failings and that no human being is "just" in his sight. Jesus, of course, was "just" because he alone was without sin. In his passion, however, the Father "made him to be sin who did not know sin, so that we might become the righteousness of God in him" (2 Corinthians 5:21).

Second, as the psalm proceeds, I tell God my condition. My soul is under attack. I am in "darkness." My "life" is crushed. My "spirit" fails. My "heart" is numb. Truly the psalmist describes a state of complete aridity of soul. I feel entirely besieged and my strength fails.

As a source of consolation, I think of times past when God was present to me. I recall what God did then. Now "I stretch out my hands" to God in an appeal for help. What is my condition? I am like a desert in need of moisture. All that I long for is the presence of God.

My prayer becomes: Hasten and help me! Without you I am like the dead. This morning, every morning, let me know that you love me. Show me how to "walk." It is in you that I "trust" and to you that I "lift up my soul." You, God, are my "refuge." All I want is to do your will because "you . . . are my God." I ask that your "good spirit guide me" on paths easy to tread. Please save "my soul from distress!"

We can pray this psalm in times of affliction, especially when we do not feel that God is near. We can hear Jesus utter this prayer during his passion. In Gethsemane, in great distress, he prayed; "Not my will but yours be done" (Luke 22:42). This psalm likewise presents the petition: "teach me to do your will." We, like Jesus, may be asked to walk a road of suffering and pain. This road is much harder if God seems to be absent. Jesus was brought to the point that he cried out "My God, my God, why have you forsaken me?" (Matthew 27:46). Without the presence of God the soul becomes truly desolate. God, however, is ever "faithful," ever "just." We should trust him always.

From a Carmelite perspective this psalm helps us to understand states of the soul where God seems to be miles away. We trust, we believe that God dwells in the center of our souls. We long to abide in his presence, to become, in deep prayer, absorbed in him. But sometimes we cannot find him! Sometimes our sins and failings, our inner "enemies," seem to get the upper hand. Then we are in darkness, "life" crushed to the ground, "spirit" failing, "heart" numb. We strive valiantly to recall what God was like in the past. Within our souls we are like a "parched land," thirsting for God's presence. He is there. We are sure that he is there. We want him to show his "face," to "answer." To be without God is like being without life. Oh, where is he? I desire to find God deep within my soul. Then I will know how to "walk." I will know God's "will." This darkness overwhelms me. Only God can save me by making his presence known.

We realize, as Carmelite writers have made clear, that we must traverse darkness such as this psalm describes. Walking in sheer faith, walking in the dark, is part of the journey of faith. But we will cry out in our pain. The experience described in the psalm makes us realize that others too have walked this road. We find consolation in the words it gives us to utter.

Canticle: Isaiah 66:10-14a

We sing this canticle in our own voice and that of the Church. We are the new Jerusalem, the Church founded by Jesus. We hear first of what this Jerusalem, our Church, is like. Then we discover that God is like this wonderful city! In the opening lines we are called on to be filled with joy and rejoicing over Jerusalem. She is like a mother ready to feed us abundantly. The Lord loves her and promises to bless her with "prosperity" and "wealth." These will flood into her. This Jerusalem will treat us like beloved children. She will above all "comfort" us. God too will "comfort" us. Receiving this treatment, our hearts will "rejoice," our bodies will "flourish."

We see in this canticle the abundant life that we will find in the Church. In Psalm 143 we suffered the apparent absence of God. We called upon him with deep longing and in great dryness of soul. In this canticle we are told where to find God. He is with his Church and he offers us overflowing "comfort." Our hearts rejoice excessively.

Psalm 147:1-11

In this psalm of praise that we render to God in our voice and that of the Church, we can find direct address adding richness to its meaning. We learn in detail who God is.

> We praise *you, Lord,* for *you are* good;
> we sing to *you, God,* for *you are* loving:
> to *you* our praise is due.

You, Lord, build up Jerusalem
and *bring* back Israel's exiles,
you heal the broken-hearted,
you bind up all their wounds.
You fix the number of the stars;
you call each one by its name.

We begin by saying to God: you are "good" and "loving." How does God show his love? You "build up Jerusalem," your Church. You *"heal"* and *"bind* up . . . wounds."* God we see as one who establishes and heals his people. What wisdom God displays! We may wonder if he can know every human being. Are we not too many for individual attention? No! God has created all the stars and "calls each" by name. If he knows so many of them, he certainly can know each of us.

Lord, you are great and almighty;
your wisdom can never be measured.
You raise the lowly;
you humble the wicked to the dust.

In these lines we recognize God's mighty nature. Human beings can never grasp his "wisdom." How does God always act? He raises up what is humble and "lowly." The proud will ever fall.

In the next lines we learn how God acts through his creation:

You cover the heavens with clouds;
you prepare the rain for the earth. . . .

You provide the beasts with their food
and young ravens that call upon *you.*

Your delight is not in horses
nor your pleasure in warriors' strength.
You delight in those who revere *you,*
in those who wait for *your* love.

God's loving care provides rain that produces food. He feeds all living creatures. He does not take "delight" in animals or humans who become mighty in their own strength. He looks for those who "revere" him and wait on his will. In these he takes "delight."

This psalm presents a consistent picture of God as one providing food and care for all living creatures. He watches how we behave. What attracts his help and what gives him joy are those who acknowledge him, who realize that, before this mighty God, they are small. He then has the joy of blessing us richly.

Reading: Romans 8:18-21

We may suffer pain and distress during our life. But we must remember that all is small in comparison to the "glory" that God will reveal to us. Paul suggests that all creation, just like human beings, suffered from the sin of Adam. But Jesus has brought hope to all of creation, both human beings and all of nature. What is held out to us is the hope of being truly free, of sharing "the glorious freedom of the children of God." Nature too, Paul suggests, will have a share in this freedom. This glorious possibility strengthens us in times of affliction.

Friday

Psalm 51

See discussion at *Week I, Friday, Morning Prayer,* p. 41.

Canticle: Tobit 13:8-11,13-15

From a Christian perspective we have in this canticle a vision of the new Jerusalem, the Church. What we find revealed in this new Jerusalem is the "Lord's majesty." "Jerusalem" is a "holy city": the Church likewise is holy. God has punished human beings for their sinful actions, but he ever has "pity" for those who are "righteous." We recognize the goodness of God. From him comes gladness. We hope that he will "cherish" us.

What is the new Jerusalem to be for the world? "A bright light." Inhabitants from all parts of the earth will find salvation in the Church. It is her role to announce the message of truth. All of us have been redeemed by the death of Jesus on the cross. We will come "bearing . . . gifts," surrendering our hearts to this God who has "so loved the world" (John 3: 16). "Through all ages forever" the Church will be the scene of praise for God. She is the "chosen one," founded to last forever.

What shall we see in the Church? "The children of the righteous" blessing God. All those who love the Church and rejoice over her prosperity will be "happy." Those who "grieve" over her "chastisements" will also come to rejoice as they see all the joy of the Church that will last forever. Truly, in every one of us, our soul blesses the wondrous God we have.

Psalm 147:12-20

See discussion at *Week II, Friday, Evening Prayer,* p. 96.

Reading: Galatians 2:19b-20

In this brief passage Paul presents the model for every Christian life. First, we are to deny the self within and come to be able to say: "I have been crucified with Christ." Second, as our self dies, a new life begins to blossom forth within us: "Christ is living" in us. We retain, of course, our human life but it is now one based on "faith in the Son of God." Why do I strive to exchange my life for that of Jesus? This Son of God "loved me and gave himself for me."

Saturday

Psalm 92

See discussion at *Week II, Saturday, Morning Prayer,* p. 98.

Canticle: Ezekiel 36:24-28

In this beautiful canticle we hear the promises that God makes to draw his people together, purifying them and sharing his life with them. We are this people, we who belong to his Church. God tells us: "I will sprinkle clean water upon you"; I will "cleanse you" from your idols, things on which you place high and undeserving value. In these images we see both an inward cleansing and a freeing from all attachments to created things. We can see in these lines a description of Christian baptism.

God promises to do more! He is going to work in our hearts. He originally created them to be "natural" hearts, but our actions, desires, and choices have changed them into "stony" hearts. He will take out these aberrations and give us instead a "new heart." He is going to give us also a "new spirit," to live within us and to direct our paths. This "spirit" is his very own! It will help us to keep his commands and decrees. With this "new heart" and "new spirit," we shall truly become God's people. In these mentions of God's "spirit," we can see references to Christian confirmation. God sends the Holy Spirit into our souls to strengthen and to guide us.

This canticle presents a wonderful picture of what the Church is for each Christian. It offers baptism by which we are cleansed of all "impurities." It offers confirmation by which we become temples of the Holy Spirit. We are now God's "people," enlivened and guided by his gifts of grace.

Psalm 8

See discussion at *Week II, Saturday, Morning Prayer,* p. 101.

Reading: 2 Peter 3:13-15a

This passage tells us what we Christians are awaiting: "new heavens and a new earth." While we are waiting, we are to strive zealously to be without sin and to be "at peace" with God. Does God seem to delay? We must see that he is patient with human beings so that more people will achieve "salvation." When the "new heavens and a new earth" appear, we shall find that justice flourishes therein.

II: Evening Prayer

Sunday, Evening Prayer I

Psalm 122

We speak this psalm in the first-person. Our voice may be our own or that of the Church. On one level we share the gladness of a group going to Jerusalem to pray in "God's house." Jerusalem is much loved because it is the seat of God's temple. In Jerusalem also "were set the thrones of judgment of the house of David." In the last two stanzas we have one urgent desire: peace. Since we are so grateful to have our holy temple, we pray for the "good" of other people.

We can hear in this psalm also the voice of Jesus. How he loved Jerusalem! How he grieved that the temple would be destroyed (Matthew 24:2). Jesus was offered in the temple as a baby (Luke 2:22). He went every year "to Jerusalem for the feast of Passover" (Luke 2:41). Like the tribes, he went up to this location of "God's house."

As the one who was to inherit "the throne of David his father" (Luke 1:32), he must have loved Jerusalem where "the thrones of judgment of the house of David" were set. Jesus is primarily the one who brings peace to the world: "Peace I leave with you; my peace I give to you" (John 14:27). Isaiah had proclaimed him: "Prince of Peace" (9:5). His prayer for us is always one of peace since he has conquered all sin and death.

From a Carmelite perspective, we say this psalm with great joy. I rejoice at the suggestion: let us pray. My focus turns to the presence of God in my soul. Soon I am before him. I am the new "Jerusalem." My soul especially is the new city where God loves to dwell. As I enter the presence of God, my one longing is for "peace." I wish peace for all peoples; I pray for their "good." My joy at knowing that God dwells within myself and others knows no bounds. Yes, truly "I rejoiced when I heard them say: 'Let us go to God's house.'"

Psalm 130

In this psalm we speak directly to God in our own voice and that of the Church. This is a psalm that rests on a deep self-awareness. We are sinners. From a Christian point of view, we say this psalm with conviction and hope. Jesus has shown us how merciful God is. He died willingly that we might be free of all sin and guilt. How we revere him!

I begin the psalm, speaking from the depth of my being: "Out of the depths I cry to you, O Lord." I plead with God to hear my cry. I say to God: "If you, Lord, should mark our guilt, Lord, who would survive?" Then with joy, I speak of God's "forgiveness." The psalmist suggests that we human beings "revere" God for this characteristic in particular: he forgives.

I then describe my soul. It "is waiting for" the Lord, trusting him. It "is longing for" the Lord, "more than

watchman for daybreak." As surely as the day will come,
God will be faithful. How do we know this? Because the
very essence of God is "mercy and fullness of redemption." He "will redeem" us from all our sins.

We begin this psalm in desperate entreaty to God. We
affirm that our cries will be heard, that "mercy and fullness of redemption" will flow from on high. We end the
psalm on a firm note of confidence: he will save us.

Canticle: Philippians 2:6-11

See discussion at *Week I, Sunday, Evening Prayer I*,
p. 51.

Reading: 2 Peter 1:19-21

The message of the gospel is one of bright, shining
light. It is "altogether reliable." It is like a "lamp" that
lightens the darkness. If we concentrate upon it, something wonderful happens within our souls. A "morning
star rises" in our hearts. The message of the gospel
becomes a living reality within our beings. We become,
as Jesus described us, "the light of the world" (Matthew
5:14). This light within comes from the presence of the
Holy Spirit who inspires people to speak.

Sunday, Evening Prayer II

Psalm 110:1-5, 7

See discussion at *Week I, Sunday, Evening Prayer II*,
p. 52.

Psalm 112

In this psalm we find a description of the person who
"fears the Lord." We see in these lines what we wish to
be and what the Church desires her children to be. Who
is happy? The person who stands in awe of God and
"takes delight in all his commands." As human beings,

we should recognize that we are creatures, made out of love by a wondrous God. In accepting who we are, we find peace. In having a personal relationship with God, we also find happiness. Once we know who God is, we wish to lead the life he plans for us: we take "delight in his commands."

The psalm tells us that blessings attend those who have faith in God. Such people exhibit "justice." In a world of injustice and darkness, they shine forth like "lights." What are these people like? "Generous, merciful and just." In exhibiting these traits, they resemble God who also is ever "generous, merciful and just."

What do these people do? They lend to those in need; they act honorably and justly. They do not fear the future because their trust is "in the Lord." They show mercy to the poor, ever acting with justice. Those who choose the path of evil feel angry at these individuals, but the strength of evil people will always fade away.

This psalm tells us that when we stand in awe of God and strive to keep his commandments we truly come to share in his life. God is ever kind, merciful, and just. Those who honor him become likewise. Such people are ever "happy" and blessed.

Canticle: Revelation 19:1-7

See discussion at *Week I, Sunday, Evening Prayer II*, p. 55.

Reading: Hebrews 12:22-24

In this passage we hear of where we Christians stand. We have become the new Israel. We have, therefore, come to the new city of God, the "heavenly Jerusalem." Who is there? God, his angels, souls "made perfect," and Jesus, the "mediator of a new covenant" whose blood has redeemed all peoples. We have become citizens of heaven and the company we share is glorious.

Monday

Psalm 136–I

This psalm is a "litany" with a response repeated after each verse: "for his love endures for ever." In performance one person would apparently speak the verse with a congregation repeating the response. The psalmist presents reason after reason for our affirming that God's love "endures for ever." In the description of every event we are to understand that God's eternal love was the operative factor. In part I of this psalm our attention is drawn to God's work in creation. God is Lord of the universe. In "wisdom" he created skies, earth, and sea. He made the "great lights," the "sun" and the "moon." All the magnificent structure of the heavens fills us with awe. We know who made it! Our response is to give endless thanks to God who loves us infinitely.

Psalm 136–II

In the second part of this psalm we focus on God's acts of salvation. We hear of his love and care for the Israelites, as he rescued them from bondage and led them into a new land. From a Christian point of view we associate these actions with our own rescue from the bondage of sin and death. Jesus has died for us, and all our sins have been forgiven. We have been carried into a new land, the Church, our safe shelter and haven from distress. The second part of Psalm 136 makes a general reference to how God acts: "He remembered us in our distress . . . and snatched us away from our foes." This he did in the past and will continue to do so. It is God who feeds all living creatures. He sustains his universe, ever redeeming and protecting it. We end the psalm as we began, giving "thanks."

Canticle: Ephesians 1:3-10

See discussion at *Week I, Monday, Evening Prayer*, p. 58.

Reading: 1 Thessalonians 3:12-13

We have heard in Psalm 136 of how God's "love endures forever." We are to imitate God, being filled to overflowing with love for all people. Paul prays that our hearts may find strength. What are they to become? "Blameless and holy" before God when Jesus returns. God can transform us, making us into the image of Jesus and giving us hearts strong in their capacity to love.

Tuesday

Psalm 137:1-6

In this psalm of lament we cry out to God in our voice and that of the Church. From the Christian point of view we long for heaven, all of us now in exile. The psalm describes the pain of those far from their beloved "Zion" and "Jerusalem." Their songs have been stilled. They cannot sing "on alien soil." Jerusalem is their highest prize; no joy can compare with her.

This psalm tells us how to love the Church, the new Jerusalem. Nothing in our lives can compare with her. Nothing is of value apart from her. In the haven of the Church we can be at peace and there we will joyfully sing. So too in the new heavenly Jerusalem our voices will ring out their praise of God.

Psalm 138

In the first psalm of this *Evening Prayer* we expressed our longing for God in his Church. In this second psalm we address God directly in our own voice and that of the Church. Our prayers have been answered and we are in God's presence. I start by thanking God "with all my heart." "I will adore" before his holy temple. What is the cause of my gratitude? God showed me "faithfulness and love." I called on God and he answered! What did he do? He "increased the strength of my soul." The psalmist exclaims that the whole earth will praise God because his ways are most glorious.

We then hear what God is like. He is "high" himself yet "he looks on the lowly." He knows well who is "haughty" and it is not such a person whom he helps. I tell God: "In the midst of affliction you give me life." When circumstances are hard and distressful, God is at the very center of them, infusing me with courage and strength. I realize: You, God, will do "all things for me!" How can this occur? God's love is "eternal." He will take care of the creatures he has made.

In this psalm we can hear the voice of Jesus, especially after the resurrection. The Father heard the words of Jesus on the cross: "Into your hands I commend my spirit" (Luke 23:46). Truly Jesus would say: "In the presence of the angels I will bless you. I will adore before your holy temple." The Father showed "faithfulness and love" and answered Jesus on the day he "called." For this action of the Father all on earth will sing: "How great is the glory of the Lord!" The Father stretched out his hand and saved Jesus. We know that his love is "eternal." "For God so loved the world that he gave his only Son, so that everyone who believes in him might not perish but might have eternal life" (John 3:16). The Father has not discarded the "work" of his hands but redeemed all human beings.

From a Carmelite perspective, we can recite this psalm deep within our souls where God dwells. Entering into prayer we "thank" God, we bless him, we "adore" before his "holy temple," found within our very beings. There we encounter a God of "faithfulness and love." From there God sends "strength" into our souls. Recognizing that God is there, we sing out: "How great is the glory of the Lord!" The God who dwells within, this mighty God, knows who is "lowly" and who is "haughty." From within I experience help from God in times of trouble. Always he is there to aid me. This God, who dwells in his "holy temple" in my soul, shows "love" that is "eternal."

Canticle: Revelation 4:11; 5:9, 10, 12

See discussion at *Week I, Tuesday, Evening Prayer*, p. 61.

Reading: Colossians 3:16

Paul urges us to let the "word of Christ" dwell in us. This word is rich and will bear fruit in love for God and neighbor. If we fill our beings with the gospel message, we will be transformed within. Our "wisdom," coming from this source, will be "made perfect." With it we can help other people. Our hearts will rejoice and we will praise God in song.

Wednesday

Psalm 139–I (1-18, 23-24)

In this psalm we pray in our own voice and in that of the Church. We address God directly and describe the close relationship we have with him. I begin by telling God how intimately he knows me. He is interested in everything I do. He searches me and "knows" me. He perceives when I sleep or rise, walk or lie down. God discerns "my purpose from afar." "All my ways lie open" to him.

Even before I act, God knows what I am going to do. God surrounds me thoroughly, laying "his hand . . . upon me." I could never understand this intimate concern for me. What if I think of fleeing from God? There is nowhere to go where he is not! He fills the heavens and the depths of the earth. Even if I go to the very end of the sea, there too I find his guidance and care. If I were to go into deepest darkness, even in that place he is present, "and the night is as clear as the day" for him.

From a Carmelite perspective, we recognize how very close God is to us in our souls. There we can feel his loving attention to our lives. He searches and "knows" me. Every one of my actions and words is known to him. He is ever present in my being in a way "too wonderful" for me to appreciate. There is no place that I can go where God is not with me. He is always within. Even if I am in great darkness, God is present in that darkness. Night to him is light.

Psalm 139–II

In this part of the psalm I speak to God explaining to myself why God is so close to me. "You . . . created my being." My being is a thing of "wonder" and for it I am grateful. You knew me from the first moment of my existence. You have seen all my actions. You know everything that I will do until the end of my days.

As I think of you, God, I realize that your thoughts are not at all like mine. They are "mysterious." If I tried to "count" them, they would be "more than the sand." If I ever tried to finish counting them, I would have to be an "eternal" being. How, then, do I wish to relate to you, God? I want you to "search me . . . and know my heart," to "test me and know my thoughts." I ask you to keep me from going the wrong way and to lead me "in the path of life eternal." Be my protector and guide always!

From a Carmelite perspective I realize even more how close God is to me. He fashioned my soul from the first moment and made it his dwelling place. It has been with me in every action and will be with me in all future actions. My divine guest is mysterious! I do not understand his thoughts, and they are too numerous to count. I wish this God who has made my soul his abode to "search me . . . and know my heart." He can purify me and guide me in the right way. I want this God to know "my thoughts." He will understand best how my mind works and guide me with his wisdom. If I learn to listen to him and discern his thoughts, I will be kept from following "the wrong path" and I will find "the path of life eternal."

Never was a God so close to his children as our God! Since he is love, we can trust him completely whether we are in joy or in distress. He is there, lending meaning to the pain and offering hope of light when all seems to be dark.

Canticle: Colossians 1:12-20

See discussion at *Week I, Wednesday, Evening Prayer*, p. 64.

Reading: 1 John 2:3-6

How can we be sure that we know Jesus? We are to follow what he taught, especially his exhortation to love. The more we keep "his word," the more love grows in us. In time the "love of God" becomes perfect in us. Imitating Jesus will bring us to "abide in him" and to be "in union with him."

Thursday

Psalm 144–I

See discussion at *Week IV, Tuesday, Morning Prayer*, p. 161.

Psalm 144–II

We continue this psalm, telling God that we will sing "a new song" to him. We recall how God rescued David from those who were his enemies. The remainder of the psalm contains prayers for our future. We hope that our children will "flourish." We would like to prosper in all

crops and herds so that our food supply will be abundant. We ask God for blessings, knowing that those are
"happy" who honor God. In this part of Psalm 144 we
ask for God's rich blessing upon us. God rescues and
gives generously. In him our hearts give thanks.

Canticle: Revelation 11:17-18; 12:10b-12a

See discussion at *Week I, Thursday, Evening Prayer,*
p. 69.

Reading: Colossians 1:23

The gospel is for all people. We have heard the good
news of our salvation. Jesus has died and risen! We
have to "hold fast to faith." We are to be "grounded" in
it and "unshaken in the hope promised" to us. This attitude of staunch belief must characterize all our actions.

Friday

Psalm 145–I

Here we have a hymn of praise that we can sing in our
own voice and that of the Church. I speak directly to
God, telling him how I plan to praise him always. I turn
my attention to the future, announcing that all ages will
praise God. Why? God works wonders. With him is
"splendor and glory." With him also we find "abundant
goodness" and "justice." How does he relate to human
beings? He is "kind and full of compassion, slow to
anger, abounding in love." What else would we ever
desire in God?

The psalmist then again looks to the future, suggest-
ing that all creation will be filled with thanksgiving.
They will recognize God's "might" and the "glory" of his
reign. We never have to fear that we will lose God. His
kingdom is "everlasting," his "rule lasts from age to
age."

Psalm 145–II

In this part of Psalm 145 we find a splendid description of different attributes of God. In his "words" God is "faithful"; in his "deeds," "loving." To whom does he direct his gaze? To those "who fall" or "are bowed down." These people he helps and saves. How does he relate to his creation? He finds all of us as we look to him. As he acts, God is "just" and "loving." Where is he to be found? "Close to all who call him, who call on him from their hearts." What does God do for us? He grants our "desires." He hears our "cry." He "saves" us and "protects" us. All people in all ages should bless this God forever.

Canticle: Revelation 15:3-4

See discussion at *Week I, Friday, Evening Prayer,* p. 72.

Reading: Romans 8:1-2

In this brief passage we find cause for great joy. Christ Jesus has saved us from all our sins. We have been redeemed! The Holy Spirit dwells within our hearts, guiding and directing our lives. We are no longer bound by a law of "sin and death." Instead, we live in Christ Jesus.

5.
Canticles of Zechariah and Mary

Let every word be Your Word, every act
a gift of mercy and grace.

I: Canticle of Zechariah

Every morning the Church has us sing the canticle that Zechariah spoke when he regained his voice at the naming of John the Baptist. This canticle, also known as the *Benedictus,* is found at Luke 1:68-79. Since Zechariah did not trust the message of the angel informing him that he would have a son, he became mute. During the nine months before the birth of John the Baptist, Zechariah had, we can assume, much time to reflect in silence on what was happening to him and Elizabeth. During the first five months Elizabeth chose to remain "in seclusion" (Luke 1:24). We can imagine these two people, quiet and secluded, experiencing and pondering upon the wonder of what God was doing in their lives.

Then, in the sixth month, a visitor arrived. Mary came from Nazareth with wonderful news! As she greeted Elizabeth, the child "leaped" in Elizabeth's womb (Luke 1:41). Elizabeth, "filled with the holy Spirit" (1:41), calls Mary "the mother of my Lord" (1:43). Mary stays with Elizabeth and Zechariah for three months. Once again, we can imagine what conversations these two women may have had about their future sons. With Zechariah also, although he could not speak, they may have reflected about who their children would be and what they would accomplish in God's plan.

The moment came for John to receive his name. Zechariah had to confirm his assent to the name "John" by using a writing tablet. Once he did so, he recovered his speech and immediately praised God in a canticle of prophecy. We can suggest, therefore, that one reason the Church has us begin every day with this canticle is that it is a song of *beginning*. God is doing wonderful, new things for his people. John the Baptist will prepare the way for Jesus and will be his herald. Each day God likewise does wonderful, new things for each of us. We too will have an important role: to prepare the way for Jesus to enter the lives and hearts of those we meet.

A second reason that the Church has us begin our day with this canticle is its rich content. This content becomes richer still if we change the passages to direct address and also if we put in specific references to Jesus wherever they are appropriate. We sing this canticle in the voice of the Church. In this voice we can discern clearly her mission to preach Christ to the world, to tell of "salvation," "forgiveness," "mercy," light, and "peace." We sing this canticle also in our own voice. In so doing we become deeply aware of the high "call" we have received (Ephesians 4:1) to take Jesus to his world. We have been endowed with dignity and honor in being chosen for such a task.

This is a task we are to take up every day, not accepting it vaguely as part of our identity as Christians, but specifically as a vital part of each of our days, consciously chosen, willingly accepted, and zealously carried out, hour by hour. We will hold our mission before us as a way in which we can become "the light of the world" and "the salt of the earth" (Matthew 5:13-14). We may not discern much progress on a particular day or over any particular period of time, but this will not concern us. What we will strive to do each day is to live the canticle of Zechariah. When evening comes, we will gratefully rest, knowing that tomorrow we will take up our task once more, urged on by the Church as it has us sing Zechariah's song.

Let us now examine this lovely song, presented here in direct address with some specific references to Jesus. We can detect in these lines the deep reflection that Zechariah may have carried on during his months of silence. We see the abundant presence of the Holy Spirit, filling Zechariah with rich inspiration.

> Blessed *are you, Lord,* the God of Israel;
> *you have* come to *your* people and set *us* free.

We bless our God who has always been with his people. He is the God of Israel. We, the Church, are the new Israel. God deserves our gratitude. We then hear of the one major action he has performed. "*You have* come . . . and set *us* free!" Here we think of the coming of Jesus and the salvation of the world. Zechariah knows that this act of salvation is happening at the very moment he speaks. Mary is carrying the child who will be called "Jesus." This child, whose name means "savior," will truly set all human beings free.

> *You have* raised up for us a mighty savior,
> *Jesus,* born of the house of *your* servant David.

Once again we hear of the savior who will be born. The angel had told Mary: "The Lord God will give him the throne of David his father" (Luke 1:32). Zechariah had heard, we can assume, what the angel told Mary. Jesus is truly a "mighty savior." He comes from the royal line of David. What else will be true of him? "He will rule over the house of Jacob forever, and of his kingdom there will be no end" (Luke 1:33).

> Through *your* holy prophets *you* promised of old
>   that *you* would save us from our enemies,
>   from the hands of all who hate us.
>
> *You* promised to show mercy to our fathers
> and to remember *your* holy covenant.

Long ago God foretold one who would save the human race. In Genesis 3:15 he promises new "offspring" that will separate us from the power of evil. He tells the serpent:

> I will put enmity between you and the woman,
> and between your offspring and hers;
> He will strike at your head,
> while you strike at his heel.

Again and again the prophets foretell the coming of an anointed one, the Messiah, to save his people. Jesus is this Messiah. As Peter tells us (Acts 10:43): "To him all the prophets bear witness about him that everyone who believes in him will receive forgiveness of sins through his name." Jesus has saved us from our greatest "enemies," our own sins. Those at work in ourselves harm us. Those at work in others cause enmity and hatred. God, however, filled with mercy, has sent us Jesus. Paul makes the situation clear:

> But God, who is rich in mercy, because of the great love he had for us, even when we were dead in our transgressions, brought us to life with Christ (by grace you have been saved), raised us up with him, and seated us with him in the heavens in Christ Jesus, that in the ages to come he might show the immeasurable riches of his grace in his kindness to us in Christ Jesus (Ephesians 2:4-7).

God established a covenant with his people on Mount Sinai (Exodus 19:5). This covenant is one that "he remembers forever" (1 Chronicles 16:15). Now, in mercy, God has established a new covenant with us. Jesus at the Last Supper says to his disciples: "This cup is the new covenant in my blood" (1 Corinthians 11:25). In Hebrews 9:15 we hear of how Jesus' death on the cross has placed us in a new covenant relationship with God:

> For this reason he is mediator of a new covenant: since a death has taken place for deliverance from transgressions under the first covenant, those who

are called may receive the promised eternal inheritance.

Zechariah tells us that God is faithful. As we sing his canticle, we know in far more detail than he how true this is.

> This was the oath *you* swore to our father Abraham:
> to set us free from the hands of our enemies,
> free to worship *you* without fear,
> holy and righteous in *your* sight all the days of our life.

Zechariah sings further of God's fidelity and mercy. When Abraham does not refuse to offer up Isaac as a sacrifice, God swears to him that his "descendants" will be plentiful and they will not be overcome by their enemies (Genesis 22:16-18). We are those "descendants" and we have been saved from the most deadly of "enemies," our own sins and failings. As Christians, we rejoice that Jesus has redeemed us and made it possible, by grace, truly to have "the glorious freedom of the children of God" (Romans 8:21). We can now be free from "fear." We can worship God, coming into his presence as his redeemed children. How does he look upon us? As "holy and righteous" people. This is what we have become "in his sight" because Jesus has washed us in his blood. We can be such "all the days of our life." Paul will give a similar description of us in our redeemed state, saying of God (Ephesians 1:4):

> as he chose us in [Christ], before the foundation of the world, to be holy and without blemish before him in love.

We may often find that we have sinned. We may not, in ourselves, seem to be "holy and righteous." Others likewise may not appear to be correctly described in this way. But this description is true, nonetheless, because in Christ we are ever "a new creation" (2 Corinthians 5:17). Paul says further (2 Corinthians 5:17-19):

The old things have passed away; behold, new things have come. And all this is from God, who has reconciled us to himself through Christ and given us the ministry of reconciliation, namely, God was reconciling the world to himself in Christ, not counting their trespasses against them and entrusting to us the message of reconciliation.

Zechariah prophesies a new condition for human beings and we fulfill his prophecy in Jesus.

The canticle now shifts attention to the child to be born, John the Baptist. Zechariah defines what he is to be called and what he is to do. By having us sing this canticle each morning, the Church assigns a similar role to us. John the Baptist was to make people ready to receive Jesus. We are to do the same.

You, my child, shall be called the prophet of the Most High;
for you will go before the Lord to prepare his way.

Isaiah had issued the cry: "Prepare the way of the LORD" (40:3). John was to do this. How can we do this? Partly by being the people described already: worshiping God "without fear," being "holy and righteous." John was such; so are we to be.

What is John's message to God's people?

To give his people knowledge of salvation
by the forgiveness of their sins.

All human beings basically long to hear one message: Your sins are forgiven. No matter what other concerns we may have in life, no matter how much we possess or have accomplished, in time of danger or at the hour of our death, one thing alone absorbs our whole attention. We recall our guilt; we long to be forgiven. God recognized that this was the basic longing of every human being. John's message, therefore, was to give the glorious promise: You are saved! You are forgiven! We too are to proclaim this message, telling all people about the sacrifice of Jesus on the cross and the salvation it brought to all. Paul tells us (Ephesians 1:7-8): "In him we have redemption by his blood, the forgiveness of transgressions, in accord with the riches of his grace that he lavished upon us." Jesus has brought to every human being the most precious gifts of "salvation" and "forgiveness of sins."

The canticle of Zechariah then tells the source of the salvation that is ours:

> In the tender compassion of our God
> the dawn from on high shall break upon us,
> to shine on those who dwell in darkness and the
>   shadow of death,
> and to guide our feet into the way of peace.

God shows "tender compassion." He has sent us Jesus, the "light of the world" (John 8:12) and giver of "peace" (John 14:27). He was foretold by Isaiah that he would be such (9:1):

> The people that walked in darkness
>   have seen a great light;
> Upon those who dwelt in the land of gloom
>   a light has shone.

The canticle of Zechariah echoes these words. Isaiah also describes the Messiah as "Prince of Peace" (9:5). Paul tells us that Jesus has brought us into a new realm of radiant brightness. He says of the Father (Colossians 1:13-14): "He delivered us from the power of darkness and transferred us to the kingdom of his beloved Son, in whom we have redemption, the forgiveness of sins."

As we begin each day, "dawn from on high" breaks upon us. We may feel that we are "in darkness" or, even more terribly, in "the shadow of death," but we encounter new brightness with each day. This brightness, arising from the "tender compassion of our God" in sending us Jesus to redeem us, ever brings us new hope and guides "our feet into the way of peace." This is our experience each morning as we say this canticle of Zechariah. This is also our message for those whom we will meet this day. We can say to them what we have learned is true for us (Isaiah 60:1):

Rise up in splendor! Your light has come,
the glory of the Lord shines upon you.

The canticle of Zechariah is a most fitting song for us to sing each morning. In its richness it presents the whole Christian message. It focuses our eyes on Jesus. It tells of the wondrous mercy of the Father. It fills us with inexpressible joy over what Jesus has done for us and made us in the sight of the Father. It urges us to take the message of salvation to all whom we meet, showing them a bright beam of hope and a cherished refuge of peace.

II: Canticle of Mary

The *Canticle of Mary*, also called the *Magnificat*, is the song of joy that Mary expressed as she greeted Elizabeth (Luke 1:46-55). We repeat her song each day at *Evening Prayer.* Mary was overwhelmed with wonder and thanksgiving at what God had done for her. So we too, looking back on our day, rejoice with gratitude at God's continuous gifts of grace.

When Mary received the message of the angel, she knew exactly what she had to do. She "traveled . . . in haste" to visit Elizabeth. As she journeyed, she must have pondered much on what she had been told:

Do not be afraid, Mary, for you have found favor with God. Behold, you will conceive in your womb and bear a son, and you shall name him Jesus. He will be great and will be called Son of the Most High, and the Lord God will give him the throne of David his father, and he will rule over the house of Jacob forever, and of his kingdom there will be no end (Luke 1:30-33).

The holy Spirit will come upon you, and the power of the Most High will overshadow you. Therefore the child to be born will be called holy, the Son of God (Luke 1:35).

What amazing words! What richness of meaning! How excited she must have been! But whom could she ever tell? Who would ever believe what was going to happen? Mary arrived at the house of Elizabeth and was astonished and delighted to hear her greeting:

Most blessed are you among women, and blessed is the fruit of your womb. And how does this happen to me, that the mother of my Lord should come to me? For at the moment the sound of your greeting reached my ears, the infant in my womb leaped for joy. Blessed are you who believed that what was spoken to you by the Lord would be fulfilled (Luke 1:42-45).

Mary then knew that she could openly share with Elizabeth what she had experienced. Her first action was to pour forth a song of praise to God who had done such amazing things in her case.

The canticle of Mary contains echoes of several Old Testament passages and especially 1 Samuel 2:1-10 wherein Hannah expresses her joy over the birth of Samuel, whom she dedicates to God. She rejoices that God mercifully has eyes for the weak and lowly and that all power is in his hands both to raise up the poor and to remove the power of the proud and haughty. In Hannah's own experience she had been treated with contempt. God heard her prayers and granted her a son. Hannah learned that God loved her. Unlike human beings who treated her with disdain, God honored her! Hannah recognized that God's ways differ greatly from those of human beings. He reverses all worldly values: what is lowly and despised he tenderly regards and cherishes.

What leads Mary to utter the song she does? We may suppose that she reflected on her own life as she traveled to Elizabeth. She may have seen other women who were proud and haughty. "God did not choose you or you," she might have thought, "but me! Yet who am I? I'm so little, so lowly. Nobody even knows who I am! I am quite insignificant." The more Mary reflected, the more clear certain things became to her. She began to see what God was really like. Just as all of us do, she may have learned much about God before this experience. Now, however, she was experiencing first hand his action in her life. What she learns about God, she will also teach her son. From her lips first Jesus will learn about a merciful and tender-hearted God.

> My soul proclaims the greatness of the Lord,
> my spirit rejoices in God my Savior
> for he has looked with favor on his lowly servant.

In these lines we see how Mary perceives herself. She is a "lowly servant." Her position is humble. Her role is to serve God. She, the chosen one, teaches us what we should be. Within, Mary's "soul" and "spirit" exult in happiness. God has favored her in a most exceptional way.

> From this day all generations will call me blessed:
> the Almighty has done great things for me,
> and holy is his Name.

Mary realizes that people will be astonished at God's choice. Mary knows that she is a lowly person, having a humble station. "Why her?" she imagines that others will ask. Mary, therefore, says: "From this day all generations will call me blessed." She knows that people will perceive that she received a remarkable blessing. When "all generations" understand that she is the mother of the Messiah, they will speak of her as truly "blessed." What has happened? "The Almighty has done great things." All praise and honor belongs to God for what he has done for Mary and for us.

Mary then speaks of God. Who is he? His essential nature is that of holiness. Mary repeats what is often asserted in the Old Testament, especially in Psalm 111:9: "Holy and awesome is your name." The "name" perfectly reflects the reality in the case of God. We see that God is essentially "holy."

In the next lines of this canticle Mary describes how the holiness of God is made manifest. In these remaining lines of this canticle, the richness of the meaning is enhanced by using direct address.

> *You have* mercy on those who fear *you*
> in every generation.

All those who love God will find him merciful. He is thus not only to a chosen few at a particular time but to all peoples always. God forgives: this is his greatest blessing for all human beings.

> *You have* shown the strength of *your* arm,
> *you have* scattered the proud in their conceit.

> *You have* cast down the mighty from their thrones,
> and *have* lifted up the lowly.

God may be hidden. He may appear silent. But God is not weak. In history he has revealed his power. Human beings may strut around in their pride. They are great, however, only in their own imaginations, in their "conceit." God does not allow them to gather and to stand firm in one place. Instead, he scatters them, all imagining that they are important and influential. Mary sees clearly that it was not one of these whom God chose to be mother of the Messiah. They might imagine that they could be chosen but in this they totally deceive themselves.

What does God do to the "mighty"? He casts them down. Whom does he lift up? The "lowly." God's ways are opposite from those of the world. Human beings honor and revere the "mighty" and despise the "lowly."

Not so God. Mary knows this to be especially true. It was not one of the "mighty" women whom God chose, but her, a "lowly handmaid."

You have filled the hungry with good things,
and the rich *you have* sent away empty.

God has an eye for the poor and needy. The "hungry" he fills. Those who are "rich" need nothing and they become "empty." In these lines we can see, in particular, a spiritual message. If we are empty, longing for spiritual gifts, God will fill us. If we are rich on any level, in possessions, attachments, pride over our gifts or achievements, self-regard or self-esteem, we cannot be filled. We will lose all these riches and find ourselves "empty." Jesus will call blessed those "who hunger and thirst for righteousness, for they will be satisfied" (Matthew 5:6). He will also tell us that those who are "poor in spirit" are likewise "blessed, for theirs is the kingdom of heaven" (Matthew 5:3). Mary recognized how God enriches with true spiritual wealth those who have made their hearts empty for him.

You have come to the help of *your* servant Israel
for *you have* remembered *your* promise of mercy,
the promise *you* made to our fathers,
to Abraham and his children for ever.

God is ever faithful. He has sent his son Jesus, as Messiah, to save human beings from sin. In doing this, God has shown himself to be merciful. What he promised of old he would do he has now done. Mary realizes that the child she carries will be a source of "help" for her people. God has now made this salvation, brought about by Jesus, available to all human beings. God's mercy, therefore, embraces all people.

In this canticle Mary reveals to us many attributes of God. His ways differ far from ours. He works in paradoxes. The "mighty" are now weak; the "lowly" rise up. The "hungry" are full; the "rich" are empty. Mary learns of these attributes by seeing how God has dealt with her. She teaches us that God deals in the same way with all people of all times. We learn a wondrous truth as we reflect on this canticle: God is like those whom he honors. Jesus' whole life will be one of lowliness and humility. He describes himself as "meek and humble of heart" (Matthew 11:29). When he speaks of rewarding those who were good, he identifies entirely with the lowly and humble people on earth: "I was hungry . . . I was thirsty . . . a stranger . . . naked . . . ill . . . in prison" (Matthew 25:31-36). Where are we to find the Messiah whom Mary bore? Like God we will find him in the poor and needy, whether they are so physically, mentally, or spiritually.

Each day the Church has us end *Evening Prayer* with the *Canticle of Mary,* the *Magnificat.* She teaches us to make this song our very own. Like Mary, we can look back over our day and see God's total gift of grace. We can be filled with joy over God's "call" to us during the day giving us a mission to fulfill. If we have met with success, we can exclaim: "The Almighty has done great things for me!" If we have had a day full of distress and difficulty, we can remember that we are God's servants. He is with us no matter how our affairs are going. We can trust him completely because he is "holy." We can see his mercy operative in our day. We see again and again how he protects and helps the humble and lowly. We can be sure that he is faithful forever. Thus our soul "proclaims the greatness of [i.e., *magnificat*] the Lord."

Select Bibliography

1. Biblical Quotations

The New American Bible, St. Joseph Edition, with revised New Testament and revised Psalms. New Jersey: Catholic Book Publishing Co., 1970, 1986, 1991.

The New Jerusalem Bible. New York: Doubleday, 1985.

2. St. Teresa of Avila

Translations:

The Collected Works of St. Teresa of Avila, trans. K. Kavanaugh, OCD and O. Rodriguez, OCD. Washington, DC: ICS Publications, 1987. 2nd ed. 3 Volumes.

The Complete Works of St. Teresa of Avila, trans. E. A. Peers. London: Sheed and Ward, 1946. 3 Volumes.

The Letters of Saint Teresa of Jesus, trans. E. A. Peers. Westminster, MD: Newman Press, 1950.

Scholarly Works:

Auclair, M., *Teresa of Avila,* trans. K. Pond. Petersham, MS: St. Bede's, 1988.

Bielecki, T., *Teresa of Avila: Mystical Writings.* New York: Crossroad, 1994.

Burrows, R., *Fire Upon the Earth: Interior Castle Explored.* Denville, NJ: Dimension, 1981.

Capalbo, B., *Praying with St. Teresa,* trans. P. Clifford. Grand Rapids, MI: Eerdmans, 1997.

Dicken, E.W.T., *The Crucible of Love: A Study of the Mysticism of St. Teresa of Jesus and St. John of the Cross.* New York: Sheed and Ward, 1963.

Dubay, T., *Fire Within: St. Teresa of Avila, St. John of the Cross and Gospel on Prayer.* San Francisco: Ignatius Press, 1989.

du Boulay, S., *Teresa of Avila: Her Story*. Ann Arbor: Hodder and Stoughton, 1991.

Frolich, M., *The Intersubjectivity of the Mystic: A Study of Teresa of Avila's "Interior Castle"*. Atlanta: Scholars Press, 1993.

Gross, F.L., *The Making of a Mystic: Seasons in the Life of Teresa of Avila*. Albany, NY: SUNY, 1993.

Howe, Elizabeth T., *Mystical Imagery: Santa Teresa de Jesús and San Juan de la Cruz*. New York: P. Lang, 1988.

Humphreys, C., *From Ash to Fire: A Contemporary Journey through the Interior Castle of Teresa of Avila*. New Rochelle: New City Press, 1992.

Luti, J. M., *Teresa of Avila's Way*. Collegeville, MN: Liturgical Press, 1991. *The Way of the Christian Mystics*, 13.

Marie-Eugene, Fr., *I Am a Daughter of the Church*. Notre Dame, IN: Fides, 1955.

_____ *I Want to See God*. Notre Dame, IN: Fides, 1953.

Medwick, C., *Teresa of Avila: The Progress of a Soul*. New York: Knopf, 1999.

Sackville-West, V., *The Eagle and the Dove (Study of St. Teresa and St. Thérèse)*. London: M. Joseph, 1943.

Slade, Carol, *St. Teresa: Author of a Heroic Life*. Berkeley: Univ. of Calif. Press, 1995.

Sullivan, Shirley D., *Transformed by Love*. Hyde Park, NY: New City Press, 2002.

Williams, R., *Teresa of Avila*. Harrisburg, PA: Morehouse Publications, 1991.

3. St. John of the Cross

Translations:

Ackerman, Jane, *The Living Flame of Love, Versions A and B*. Binghamton, NY: Medieval and Renaissance Texts and Studies, 1995.

Campbell, Roy, *Poems of St. John of the Cross*. New York: Pantheon, 1951.

Jones, K., *The Poems of St. John of the Cross, English and Spanish*. Tunbridge Wells: Burns and Oates, 1993.

Kavanaugh, K., OCD and Rodriguez, O., OCD, *The Complete Works of St. John of the Cross*. Washington, DC: ICS Publications, 1991.

Krabhenhoft, K., *The Poems of St. John of the Cross*. New York: Harcourt, Brace and Co., 1999.

Peers, E. A., *The Complete Works of Saint John of the Cross*. London: Burns and Oates, 1964. 3 Vols.

Ruiz, A., OCD, *The Prayers of John of the Cross*. Hyde Park, NY: New City Press, 1991.

Steuart, J., SJ, *The Mystical Doctrine of St. John of the Cross*, trans. D. Lewis. London: Sheed and Ward, 1974.

Scholarly Works:

Burrows, R., *Ascent to Love: The Spiritual Teaching of St. John of the Cross*. Denville, NJ: Dimension Books, 1987.

Collings, Ross, *John of the Cross*. Collegeville, MN: Liturgical Press, 1990. *The Way of the Christian Mystics*, 10.

Crisógono, de Jesús Sacramentado, Fr., *The Life of St. John of the Cross*, trans. K. Pond. New York: Harper, 1958.

Cummins, Norbert, OCD, *An Introduction to St. John of the Cross*. Darlington: Darlington Carmel, 1986.

Dicken, E.W.T., *The Crucible of Love: A Study of the Mysticism of St. Teresa of Jesus and St. John of the Cross.* New York: Sheed and Ward, 1963.

Doohan, L., *Contemporary Challenge of St. John of the Cross.* Washington, DC: ICS Publications, 1995.

Dubay, T., *Fire Within: St. Teresa of Avila, St. John of the Cross, and the Gospel on Prayer.* San Francisco: Ignatius Press, 1989.

Hardy, R.P., *Search for Nothing: The Life of St. John of the Cross.* New York: Crossroad, 1989.

Howe, Elizabeth T., *Mystical Imagery: Santa Teresa de Jesús and San Juan de la Cruz.* New York: P. Lang, 1988.

Kavanaugh, K., *John of the Cross: Doctor of Light and Love.* New York: Crossroad, 1999.

_____ *John of the Cross, Selected Writings.* New York: Paulist Press, 1987.

_____ *God Speaks in the Night: The Life, Times and Teaching of St. John of the Cross.* Washington, DC: ICS Publications, 1991.

Lewis, D., *Life of St. John of the Cross.* London: T. Baker, 1997.

Marie-Eugene, Fr., OCD, *I Am a Daughter of the Church.* Notre Dame, IN: Fides, 1955.

Matthew, I., *The Impact of God: Soundings from St. John of the Cross.* London: Hodder and Stoughton, 1995.

Muto, S., *John of the Cross for Today: The Ascent.* Notre Dame, IN: Ave Maria Press, 1991.

Paul-Marie of the Cross, OCD, *Carmelite Spirituality in the Teresian Tradition.* Washington, DC: ICS Publications, 1997.

Payne, S., *John of the Cross and the Cognitive Value of Mysticism.* Dordrecht: Kluwer Academic Publishers, 1990.

Stein, E., *The Science of the Cross. A Study of St. John of the Cross.* Chicago: Henry Regnery, 1960.

Tavard, G.H., *Poetry and Contemplation in St. John of the Cross.* Athens: Ohio Univ., 1988.

Tillyer, D.B., *Union with God: The Teaching of St. John of the Cross.* London: Mowbray, 1984.

Welch, J., *When Gods Die: An Introduction to John of the Cross.* New York, 1990.

Wojtyla, Karol. *Faith According to St. John of the Cross,* trans. J. Aumann. San Francisco: Ignatius Press, 1981.

4. Blessed Elizabeth of the Trinity

Translations:

The Complete Works of Elizabeth of the Trinity, Vol. I, trans. by A. Kane. Washington, DC: ICS Publications, 1984.

The Complete Works of Elizabeth of the Trinity, Vol. II, trans. by A.E. Nash. Washington, DC: ICS Publications, 1995.

Scholarly Works:

Balthasar, Hans Urs von, *Two Sisters in the Spirit: Thérèse of Lisieux and Elizabeth of the Trinity.* San Francisco: Ignatius Press, 1992.

Borriello, Luigi, trans. J. Aumann, *The Spiritual Doctrine of Blessed Elizabeth of the Trinity, Apostolic Contemplative.* New York: Alba House, 1986.

De Meester, C., OCD, trans. A. Kane, OCD, *Elizabeth of the Trinity, Light, Love, Life.* Washington, DC: ICS Publications, 1987.

Philipon, M.M., OP., *The Spiritual Doctrine of Sister Elizabeth of the Trinity.* Westminster, MD: Newman Press, 1947.

Sullivan, Shirley D., *Transformed by Love.* Hyde Park, NY: New City Press, 2002.

5. The Liturgy of the Hours

Editions:

Christian Prayer. New York: Catholic Book Publishing Co., 1976. Abbreviated 1 vol. version.

The Liturgy of the Hours. New York: Catholic Book Publishing Co., 1975. 4 vols.

Peoples' Companion to the Breviary. Indianapolis: Carmelites, 1997. 2 vols.

Psalms: Morning and Evening. Chicago: Archdiocese of Chicago, 1995.

Scholarly Works:

Baltzer, R.A., and Fassler, M.E., *The Divine Office in the Later Middle Ages. Studies in Honor of R. Steiner.* New York: Oxford Univ. Press, 2000.

Bradshaw, P., *Daily Prayer in the Early Church: A Study of the Origin and Early Development of the Divine Office.* London: Alciun Club, 1981.

Brook, John, *The School of Prayer: An Introduction to the Divine Office for All Christians.* Collegeville, MN: Liturgical Press, 1992.

Campbell, Stanislaus, *From Breviary to Liturgy of Hours: The Structural Reform of the Roman Office.* Collegeville, MN: Liturgical Press, 1995.

Dalmais, I.H., trans. M.J. O'Connell, *The Liturgy and Time.* Collegeville, MN: Liturgical Press, 1986.

Dix, G., *The Shape of the Liturgy.* London: Dacre Press, 1945.

Elliott, Peter J., *Ceremonies of the Modern Roman Rite: The Eucharist and the Liturgy of the Hours.* San Francisco: Ignatius Press, 1995.

Guiver, George, *Company of Voices: Daily Prayer and the People of God.* New York: Pueblo, 1988.

Irwin, Kevin W., *Advent and Christmas: A Guide to the Eucharist and Hours.* New York: Pueblo, 1986.

_____ *Context and Text: Method in Liturgical Theology.* Collegeville, MN: Liturgical Press, 1994.

_____ *Lent: A Guide to the Eucharist and Hours.* New York: Pueblo, 1985.

Jurgens, W.A., *General Instruction in the Liturgy of the Hours.* Collegeville, MN: Liturgical Press, 1975.

Little, Vilma G., *The Sacrifice of Praise: An Introduction to the Meaning and Use of the Divine Office.* London: Longmans, Green and Co., 1957.

Parsch, P., trans. W. Nayden and C. Hoegerl, *The Breviary Explained.* St. Louis: Herder, 1954.

Roguet, A.M., OP., *The Liturgy of the Hours.* London: G. Chapman, 1971.

Salmon, P., *The Breviary Through the Centuries.* Collegeville, MN: Liturgical Press, 1986.

Van Dijk, S.J.P., ed., *Sources of the Modern Roman Liturgy.* Leiden: E.J. Brill, 1963.

Van Dijk, S.J.P., and Walker, J.H., *The Origins of the Modern Roman Liturgy: The Liturgy of the Papal Court and the Franciscan Order in the Thirteenth Century.* London: Darton, Longman and Todd, 1960.

Index of Passages Discussed